WAR PLAYS

Keith Dewhurst

WAR PLAYS

THE WORLD TURNED UPSIDE DOWN

THE BOMB IN BREWERY STREET

CORUNNA!

OBERON BOOKS
LONDON

First published in 1996 by Oberon Books Ltd (incorporating Absolute Classics)
521 Caledonian Road, London N7 9RH.
Tel: 0171 607 3637/Fax: 0171 607 3629

ISBN 1 870259 63 7

Cover design: Andrzej Klimowski

Cover typography: Richard Doust

Printed by Rexam Digital Imaging Limited, Reading

CONTENTS

INTRODUCTION, 7

THE WORLD TURNED UPSIDE DOWN, 11

THE BOMB IN BREWERY STREET, 103

CORUNNA!, 207

INTRODUCTION

I must confess that until it was pointed out to me by the publisher James Hogan that what he wanted to print here was a trio of War Plays, I had never considered them in that light. As history plays, yes; I had thought of them in that way, because my novel *Captain of the Sands* and numerous plays for television and the theatre were about England's past and how to come to terms with it. What values from the energy of greatness might provide sustenance in decline? How far should we who have benefitted from wrongs feel guilty? Is it ever possible to control life's jumbled progress? And if the most agonizing thing is the destruction of what is organic and took many centuries to grow, is not the most pernicious the way in which a selfish refusal to change can be cloaked in a philosophy of educated regrets?

These are questions that someone of my age *would* ask, because when I was born the map of the world was nearly a quarter of it red for England's empire, and the myths of our island history were intact. I am not ashamed to admit that I have many times been seduced by them. *Corunna!*, for example, is about the ordinary people who bear the pains of history, and yet I still believe in Sir John Moore as a hero, and am moved by the notion that when the character Mrs Hudson is draped, almost as an act of mockery, in her dead husband's uniform, she becomes thereby the officer and is obeyed. The ambiguity of this metaphor came from my own feelings, which have still not managed to resolve themselves.

I hate war but I believe in soldiers, because I am sure that they have many times saved what is civilised and decent. I don't know whether I would be brave myself, because the most that I have done is lie in an air-raid shelter and hear the German bombers as they passed overhead, but I admire bravery and self-sacrifice in other people. I think that the notion that there is no such thing as society, and no sacrifice that is worth making for it, is contemptible and will destroy everything.

In all these plays there are characters who hold that the most important things inevitably entail sacrifices, and among those characters I would include the Provisional IRA: they are lightly touched upon, it is true, but without them the black comedy of *The Bomb in Brewery Street* has no meaning. Other characters, like Father Bogan in *The Bomb in Brewery Street*, and Gerard Winstanley in *The World Turned Upside Down*, pose other questions. Does violence impel change or retard it? Is it a part of our nature that we must live with, or one that we can and should seek to overcome?

Corunna! was the first of these plays to be performed, and I had my original idea for it in the early 1950s, when I saw the Robert Burns ballad-opera *The Jolly Beggars* on television. About ten years later I was asked by Stella Richman at ATV to submit an idea for a Christmas drama, and I wrote an outline of *Corunna!* which included the lyric for Johnny Trap's Lullaby; but nothing came of the project until 1971, as a result of my collaborations with Bill Bryden and our friendship with the folk musicians of Steeleye Span. The play was written for five actors and five band members, and we played a week at the Theatre Upstairs, and a tour of one-night stands in folk-rock venues, from theatres to concert halls and student unions. Bill re-staged the play for each new space. It had been conceived as drama outside the proscenium arch, that would assume the frontal energy of a concert by using the band's front-man as Narrator: a major step along our road to full promenade plays like *Lark Rise*. Anyone interested in the music can hear most of it on the Steeleye album *Please to See the King*, although in my opinion the track that sounds most like the live band is *Wasn't I Pretty When I Entered Cork City* on *Ten Man Mop*. In *Corunna!* this was the tune for O'Riordan's Song in the Snow Flurries.

The Bomb in Brewery Street grew out of two trips I made to Ulster in the winter of 1971. In the media war for the people's hearts and minds there were Public Relations Officers at Battalion level, and it was possible to get very close to the ground. I prevailed upon the hospitality of the Royal Scots, which had been my father's regiment in the Battle of the Somme, and my first draft ideas were written for television. They ranged too widely, and I came to realise that I should not write a play about the Irish, but one about the English in Ireland.

This was produced in its present form because it happened to be read by the actor Jack Shepherd, who recommended it to someone else: David Leland, then at the outset of his career as a director. Not the least virtue of his splendid production was that it led to lasting friendships with the actor John Salthouse and David himself.

Some reviewers of the time complained that the play was a-political and neither explained Irish history nor suggested an answer to its problems. Twenty years later the answer is still being sought, and there have been fly-on-the-wall documentaries about the armed services that are as irreverent as my own findings. Whether this would change any opinions I do not know, although mine is still the same: in a work for the theatre, which must also entertain, one sentence of truthful reportage, as when the squaddies call the Irish "wogs in houses", is in the long run more telling than an hour of polemic.

The World Turned Upside Down was written in 1978 for the superb acting company that Bill Bryden had assembled at the National Theatre: it is worth noting that three of them, plus the musicians Ashley Hutchings and Maddy Prior, had appeared in *Corunna!* It was Bill's idea that I should adapt Christopher Hill's wonderful book, and he knew that for a long time in the 1960s I had tried to write a play about Oliver Cromwell; the Burford material in the present play is taken from those earlier drafts. The play had an unfortunate production period, in which time was lost to an industrial dispute between the National Theatre and its stage technicians, and in consequence our first night was very rocky. Many reviews reflected this, which was a pity because when the production had settled down it represented in my opinion the best work that Bill Bryden, Sebastian Graham-Jones and I achieved together. The direction had immense elegance and energy on a traverse stage, and the acting was very strong. Mark McManus, an under-regarded great actor if ever there was one, was luminous as Winstanley, Toibin was a storm-cloud of a Cromwell, and Shepherd and Bob Hoskins were, of course, made by nature to lead a rebel army. The issues of the play remain among the most fascinating that any writer of historical stories can tackle.

When I lived in Sydney in the 1980s I took time to cut two scenes from *The World Turned Upside Down* and rewrite another, work that I like to think I would have done anyway if there had been preview time. In *Corunna!* people can re-date the flash-forward or not, as they see fit. These things apart, the texts of all three plays are as first performed.

When I read them again after twenty or more years they seem to me to be period pieces in one regard only: they were written in the 1970s, when bi-partisan arts policies had not been disdained, and recession had not seemed to justify the down-grading of subsidies, so that even provincial theatres could afford to mount high-risk new plays with large casts and larger dreams. In this, whatever their faults, these War Plays aspire to our theatre's old, epic, popular tradition; which has renewed itself many times and will do so again, one may be sure, even in the Century of the Super-Highway.

Keith Dewhurst
London, 1996

THE WORLD TURNED UPSIDE DOWN

freely adapted from the book by

CHRISTOPHER HILL

CHARACTERS

On the Royalist side

KING CHARLES I
BISHOP JUXON

New model army

SIR THOMAS FAIRFAX
OLIVER CROMWELL
CAPTAIN KIRBY
CAPTAIN JONES
CORNET SMITH
ROBERT LOCKYER
HENRY DEAN
CAPTAIN WILLIAM THOMPSON
CORPORAL CHURCH
TROOPER SEDLEY
MYLES SYNDERCOMBE
COLONEL HACKER
MUSKETEER OFFICER

Diggers

GERARD WINSTANLEY
WILLIAM EVERARD
RICHARD MAIDLEY
STEWER
COLTON
JOHN TAYLOR
MRS MAIDLEY
MRS COLTON
A DUMB GIRL

On the road

FURIOSITY
THEOBALD
LUCINDA
SNAPJOINT
A BEGGAR

The religious

REV JOHN PORDAGE
LUCY
ABIEZER COPPE

Ranters

MIDDLETON
MRS MIDDLETON
BAUTHUMLEY
COPPIN
JACKSON
MRS CLARKSON
LAWRENCE CLARKSON

Others

LADY ELEANOR DAVIES
MR EYRES
MRS ASHLEY
JOAN
EXECUTIONER
Crowd, Voices, Soldiers Etc.

The World Turned Upside Down was first performed at the Cottesloe Theatre on November 2nd, 1978, with the following cast:

KING CHARLES I, SEDLEY, BAUTHUMLEY
Gawn Grainger

BISHOP JUXON, A BEGGAR, FURIOSITY
Howard Goorney

SIR THOMAS FAIRFAX, MAIDLEY, MIDDLETON
Oliver Cotton

OLIVER CROMWELL, TAYLOR, THEOBALD
Niall Toibin

CAPTAIN KIRBY, WILLIAM EVERARD
Bob Hoskins

HENRY DEAN, COLTON, CAPTAIN JONES
Peter Armitage

ROBERT LOCKYER, ABIEZER COPPE, JACKSON
David Rintoul

CAPTAIN THOMPSON, LAWRENCE CLARKSON
Jack Shepherd

COL. HACKER, CORP. CHURCH, SNAPJOINT
Brian Glover

MYLES SYNDERCOMBE, JOHN PORDAGE, COPPIN
Frederick Warder

GERARD WINSTANLEY, MUSKETEER OFFICER
Mark McManus

MR EYRES, STEWER
Norman Tyrrell

MRS MAIDLEY
June Watson

MRS ASHLEY, MRS STEWER
Edna Dore

SIMPLE MIND, LUCY
Irene Gorst

LUCINDA
Maddy Prior

MRS COLTON, MRS MIDDLETON
Tamara Hinchco

MRS CLARKSON, LADY ELEANOR DAVIES
Marty Cruickshank

Other parts were played by members of the company. Mr Ashton, a part cut from this version, was played by Trevor Ray. The parts of CORNET SMITH, JOAN and the LANDLORD are new to this version.

The musicians, most of whom also appeared on stage, were Ashley Hutchings, John Tams, Michael Gregory, Peter Bullock, Maddy Prior and Keith Thompson.

DIRECTOR
Bill Bryden and Sebastian Graham-Jones

DESIGNER
William Dudley

LIGHTING
Brian Ridley

MUSICAL DIRECTORS
Ashley Hutchings, John Tams

SCENES

PROLOGUE: WHITEHALL (January 30 1649)

SCENE ONE: DIGGERS (April 1649)

SCENE TWO: MUTINY (April 25 1649)

SCENE THREE: DEBENTURES (May 1649)

SCENE FOUR: BURFORD (May 14 1649)

SCENE FIVE: MRS ASHLEY'S (May 14 1649)

SCENE SIX: CROMWELL'S SALVATION (May 15 1649)

SCENE SEVEN: BURFORD CHURCHYARD (May 15 1649)

INTERVAL

SCENE EIGHT: BRADFIELD RECTORY (Summer 1649)

SCENE NINE: ARMY HEADQUARTERS (Summer 1649)

SCENE TEN: THE ROAD TO LONDON (September 30 1649)

SCENE ELEVEN: GOLDSMITHS HALL (October 1649)

SCENE TWELVE: A VOTE TAKEN (October 1649)

SCENE THIRTEEN: WET WASHING (November 1649)

SCENE FOURTEEN: COBHAM (November 1649)

SCENE FIFTEEN: CHESTER (December 1649)

SCENE SIXTEEN: THE RANT (December 1649)

SCENE SEVENTEEN: BLASPHEMY (August 1650)

SCENE EIGHTEEN: PIRTON (September 1650)

PROLOGUE

A galliard, stately and sombre. The entire cast cloaked and romantic. Then the music becomes drumming. The actors remove their cloaks. The dance becomes a tableau: the scaffold onto which KING CHARLES I has stepped for execution.

It is a bitterly cold day: white, icy rigour and distress.

CHARLES is a little stooped and worn. His hair and beard are streaked with grey. His clothes are rich and beautiful. He wears two linen shirts, one with blue and red bows, a red striped silk waistcoat brocaded in silver and yellow, black satin doublet and breeches, and a black velvet coat. He wears pearl ear-drops. the George Star, and the Garter ribbon.

BISHOP WILLIAM JUXON accompanies the KING. He is 66 years old and in full Anglican robes.

The buffcoated COLONEL HACKER is in command of the scaffold.

The executioners wear woollen frocks and frieze breeches. They have black masks, wigs and false beards. That of the EXECUTIONER is grey. His ASSISTANT wears a black beard and a black hat turned up at the front.

There are other officers and shorthand writers. Halberdiers stand guard all round. The drums stop.

There is a low block. The KING inspects it. He is determined not to shiver in the cold. When he speaks it is with a Scots lilt.]

CHARLES: Is there a higher block?

HACKER: No.

[*The King takes from his pocket a piece of paper on which he has written notes for his speech.*]

CHARLES: I could hold my peace very well, if I did not think that holding my peace would make some men think that I did submit to the guilt as well as the punishment. But I think it is my duty to God first, and to my country, for to clear myself, both as an honest man, and as a good King, and an honest Christian.

[*From time to time voices from the crowd punctuate the speech with memories of how members of their class were born and buried.*]

VOICE: Buried: a poor young woman that was found dead in a ditch in a field of Randal Candland's near Edge Mill.

CHARLES: I shall begin first with my innocence.

VOICE: Christened: a bastard born in an outhouse in Charlton Lane.

CHARLES: In truth, I think it is not very needful for me to insist long upon innocence, for all the world knows that I never did begin a war with the two Houses of Parliament. And I call God to witness, to whom I must shortly make an account, that I never did intend for to encroach upon their privileges. They began upon me. It is the Militia they began upon. They confessed that the Militia was mine but they thought fit to have it from me.

VOICE: Paid: to a poor woman in Bulkeley that had leprosy all over her: two shillings.

CHARLES: If anybody will look at the dates of the Commissions – of their Commissions and mine – and likewise to the Declarations, he will see clearly that they began these unhappy troubles, not I. So that, as to the guilt of those enormous crimes that are laid against me, I hope in God that God will clear me of it. I will not. I am in charity.

VOICE: Christened: Roger, son of a poor woman brought to bed and delivered in a barn of Owen Goodman of Duckerton.

CHARLES: What I have said so far is to show that I am an innocent man. Now for to show you that I am a good Christian. I hope that this good man [*He indicates Juxon.*] will bear witness that I have forgiven all the world and even those in particular that would have been the chief cause of my death.

VOICE: Buried: a young woman, a stranger, found dead in a field near Otterspool.

CHARLES: I pray God with St Stephen that my death be not laid to their charge. Nay, not only so, but that they may take the right way to the peace of the Kingdom, for my charity commands me to endeavour to the last gasp the peace of the Kingdom.

[*The EXECUTIONER'S ASSISTANT fidgets with the axe.*]

Hurt not the axe that it may not hurt me.

[*CHARLES returns to his speech.*]

For the people, truly I desire their freedom and liberty as much as anybody whomsoever. But I must tell you, their liberty and freedom consists in having government – those laws by which their life and their goods may be most their own. It is not having a share in government. That is nothing pertaining to them. A subject and a sovereign are clean different things, and therefore, until they do that – I mean that you put the people in that liberty as I say – certainly they will never enjoy themselves. It is for this that I am now come here. If I would have given way to an arbitrary power, for to have all laws changed according to the power of the sword, I need not have come here. And therefore I tell you, and I pray God it be not laid to your charge, that I am the martyr of the people.

VOICE: Buried: Harry Ap Robert, a poor man coming out of Rythland in Wales: and because he was a stranger and sick nobody would lodge him. And therefore he crept into an outhouse at night and there died.

CHARLES: I have delivered my conscience. I pray God that you do take those courses which are best for the good of the Kingdom, and your own salvation.

JUXON: Will your Majesty – though it may very well be known your Majesty's affections towards religion – yet it may be expected you should say somewhat for the world's satisfaction.

CHARLES: I thank you very heartily, my lord. I declare before you all that I die a Christian according to the profession of the Church of England as I found it left me by my father. And this honest man will witness it. I have a good cause and I have a gracious God. I will say no more. Is there a block at which I can kneel?

HACKER: No. There's not one in the Tower of London.

CHARLES: Then see it is set fast.

[*He is shown the axe. He almost feels the edge but restrains himself.*]

Have a care of the axe.

[*CHARLES gives JUXON his cloak, and the star of the George.*]

Remember.

VOICE: Resolved: that the people are, under God, the origins of all just power: that the Commons of England in Parliament assembled, being chosen by and representing the people, have the supreme power in this nation.

[*CHARLES gives JUXON his ring and prayer book. JUXON gives him the cap. It is linen, with the edge turned up to form a deep border. It is embroidered with fruit and flowers. CHARLES pushes his hair up underneath it.*]

CHARLES: Is any of my hair in the way now?

EXECUTIONER: I beg you push it more under your cap.

JUXON: You have but one stage more. It is turbulent and troublesome, but it is a short one, though it will carry you a very great way. It will carry you from earth to heaven.

CHARLES: I am going from a corruptible to an incorruptible crown, where no disturbance can be.

[*The EXECUTIONER kneels.*]

EXECUTIONER: Sir: I ask your pardon.

CHARLES: The King cannot pardon a subject who wilfully sheds his blood. I pray you, do not put me to pain.

[*CHARLES moves to the edge of the scaffold. He seems about to speak again but does not. He smiles sadly as he looks down Whitehall to the Palace of his youth. Then he turns back.*]

I shall say but a short prayer, and when I hold out my hands thus, strike.

[*CHARLES stands for a moment in prayer. Then he lies down. The drums roll again. After a moment CHARLES stretches out his hands. The axe rises and falls. The crowd cry out. The EXECUTIONER'S ASSISTANT holds up*]

the severed head. The drums stop. In the silence GERARD
WINSTANLEY cries out.]

WINSTANLEY: The old world is running up like
   parchment in the fire!

SCENE ONE

DIGGERS
April, 1649

The DIGGERS advance across the stage, clearing and sowing
the land, and singing.

DIGGERS:

The gentry are all round, stand up now, stand up now
The gentry are all round, stand up now
The gentry are all round, on each side they are found
Their wisdom's so profound, to cheat us of our ground
Stand up now, stand up now
Your houses they pull down, stand up now, stand up now
Your houses they pull down, stand up now
Your houses they pull down, to fright poor men in town
But the gentry must come down, and the poor shall
   wear the crown
Stand up now, stand up now
The clergy they come in, stand up now, stand up now
The clergy they come in, stand up now
The clergy they come in, and say it is a sin
That we should now begin our freedom for to win
Stand up now diggers all.

[*When they have gone their leaders WINSTANLEY and*
EVERARD are left in the Palace of Westminster. An

*OFFICER enters, followed by the Lord General of the Army,
SIR THOMAS FAIRFAX.*]

OFFICER: Hats off. Get your hats off.

EVERARD: I'll uncover for no fellow creature.

OFFICER: This is Sir Thomas Fairfax, Lord General of
the Army. Get your hats off.

[*Silence. The OFFICER is indignant. He moves forward
to snatch the hats, but FAIRFAX checks him.*]

FAIRFAX: Let it rest, Captain.

[*The CAPTAIN steps back. FAIRFAX looks at the two
men. EVERARD has an army coat.*]

Which of you is William Everard?

EVERARD: I am.

FAIRFAX: You were in the army.

EVERARD: I was.

FAIRFAX: You were an elected Agitator, you were
involved in mutinies, and you were cashiered.

EVERARD: I am a prophet of the race of the Jews. The
liberties of the people were lost by the coming in of
William the Conqueror, and ever since we have lived
under tyranny and oppression worse than our
forefathers under the Egyptians.

FAIRFAX: You must be Mr Winstanley.

WINSTANLEY: I am.

EVERARD: But now the time of deliverance is at hand.
God will bring his people out of this slavery, and
restore them to their freedom in enjoying the fruits
and benefits of the earth.

FAIRFAX: Thank you. Information being laid before the Council of State, I was commanded to investigate. I sent a Captain and four men, who invited you to London of your own free will and reported to me as follows: on Sunday April First six soldiers pulled the preacher out of the pulpit of Walton-on-Thames church. They burnt bibles etcetera etcetera... Well, we've seen plenty of that... On the same day you, William Everard, and four other men began digging on the common land on the side of St George's Hill next to Camp Close...

EVERARD: We did.

FAIRFAX: You sowed parsnips, carrots, and beans, and on Monday you were joined by more people. On Tuesday you burned off forty rood of heath. On Friday twenty or thirty people dug all day.

EVERARD: They did: and pulled the plough.

FAIRFAX: On Saturday you bought seed corn at Kingston and abused the local people.

EVERARD: I did not.

FAIRFAX: I think so.

EVERARD: I said that if any cattle came near the plantation I'd cut their legs off.

FAIRFAX: Yesterday, April Nineteenth, my soldiers saw twenty people there, some of them women, and you'd built shelters.

EVERARD: We have.

FAIRFAX: Did you tell the soldiers that you'd pull down the palings around all rich men's lands?

EVERARD: I promised meat, drink and clothes. I said that I'd make people work.

FAIRFAX: Is that what you intend?

WINSTANLEY: Our intention is to restore the creation to its former condition.

EVERARD: Within ten days we shall be five thousand in number.

[*This produces a reaction among the officers.*]

WINSTANLEY: If we restore the ancient community of the fruits of the earth, God will make barren land fruitful.

EVERARD: What I promised was the benefits thereof to the poor and needy.

FAIRFAX: Will you meddle with property?

WINSTANLEY: No.

FAIRFAX: Will you break down pales and enclosures?

WINSTANLEY: No.

EVERARD: What we will meddle with is common and untilled land.

WINSTANLEY: One half of England is not properly cultivated, yet everywhere there are beggars and distress.

FAIRFAX: There's been a civil war and two bad harvests.

EVERARD: We've been oppressed for centuries.

WINSTANLEY: We will make untilled land fruitful for the use of man.

FAIRFAX: What men?

WINSTANLEY: All men. Men will give up their lives and estates. They will give their lives to this community.

FAIRFAX: Could you feed five thousand? Can you feed yourselves?

WINSTANLEY: Meat, drink and clothing were all promised.

FAIRFAX: But you'd have to buy food for five thousand.

EVERARD: The time of deliverance is at hand.

WINSTANLEY: We have chosen the Lord God Almighty to be our King and Protector. There is no need of money, nor of clothes, except to cover nakedness.

[*The OFFICERS are amused by what they consider to be wild crankiness. FAIRFAX is more interested and sophisticated.*]

FAIRFAX: But, surely, you use money yourselves to buy seeds and tools?

WINSTANLEY: True religion and undefiled is to let everyone quietly have earth to manure.

FAIRFAX: Suppose you spend all your money. How long will your plantation survive?

[*Silence. EVERARD almost strolls away. He laughs to himself at FAIRFAX's obtuseness. FAIRFAX accepts the reaction and pursues his point.*]

How can any of us live without trade and wages?

WINSTANLEY: He that works for another, either for wages or to pay him rent, works unrighteously; but they that are resolved to work and eat together, making the earth a common treasure, join hands with Christ to lift up the creation from bondage, and restore all things from the curse.

FAIRFAX: Would you use arms to defend yourselves?

WINSTANLEY: No.

FAIRFAX: What would you do?

WINSTANLEY: Submit to authority.

EVERARD: The promised opportunity is not at hand.

WINSTANLEY: We shall wait until it is offered.

FAIRFAX: In your tents?

EVERARD: Our Jewish forefathers lived in tents. It is suitable to our condition now to do the same.

[*FAIRFAX nods. He turns to the OFFICER.*]

FAIRFAX: Captain, have you any questions?

[*The OFFICER cannot resist.*]

OFFICER: You keep your hats on. Why?

WINSTANLEY: The Lord General is our fellow creature.

OFFICER: What is the meaning of the phrase "Give honour to those to whom honour is due"? Or don't you know?

EVERARD: I know – and their mouths should be stopped that thought of a notion so offensive.

[*The OFFICER is angry but FAIRFAX checks him.*]

FAIRFAX: Thank you, Captain. Mr Winstanley: where are you from?

WINSTANLEY: Wigan.

FAIRFAX: What's your trade?

WINSTANLEY: Clothier. I came to London as an apprentice and then set up on my own. I failed. These last bad years I've been a cowhand.

FAIRFAX: So you've known what it is to be a man with worldly goods.

WINSTANLEY: I have.

[*FAIRFAX is interested in this – and probably guessed it – but his only comment on it is a momentary silence.*]

FAIRFAX: Thank you. Thank you, Mr Everard. I'll not detain you.

[*WINSTANLEY and EVERARD exchange glances.*]

No laws have been broken and very little harm done. Good day.

[*WINSTANLEY and EVERARD go.*]

That Everard is no better than a madman.

OFFICER: He should be locked up with the other Leveller scum.

FAIRFAX: Of course he should: but he's not broken any laws yet, has he?

SCENE TWO

MUTINY
April 25, 1649

It is midnight. A group of soldiers from COLONEL WHALLEY's Dragoons burst into the galleried yard of the Bull Inn, Bishopsgate, London. They are led by the 23-year-old ROBERT LOCKYER, and CORPORAL CHURCH, a common soldier named SEDLEY, a DRUMMER and another MUSICIAN.

LOCKYER: Smith? Where are you? Cornet Smith?

[*The LANDLORD appears, very angry.*]

LANDLORD: Stop this drunken rubbish!

SEDLEY: Where's the Cornet?

LANDLORD: In his chamber.

LOCKYER: Get him out.

LANDLORD: Who are you? Who sent you?

LOCKYER: Smith! Wake up! All men of Whalley's Dragoons! Wake up!

LANDLORD: Listen, young man – I was sworn blind that all troops in this inn would be well-behaved!

LOCKYER: Nay, we do not seek to disturb any man.

CHURCH: Hey. [*Indicating the LANDLORD.*] He's locked the doors.

LOCKYER: Ignore him. He's our brother even in darkness. Smith! Come out! Where are you?

[*CORNET SMITH appears on the gallery. He has just woken up.*

A wench is with him. Her name is JOAN. Other soldiers and women appear from other rooms to see what the noise is about.]

SMITH: What's your shouting? Who are you?

LOCKYER: Robert Lockyer. Come down.

SMITH: What d'you mean? What's happened?

LOCKYER: I want the flag. Come down.

SMITH: You address an officer as sir.

CHURCH: You weren't born an officer. You were a joiner.

SMITH: Corporal: are you in command of these men?

CHURCH: No.

SMITH: You mean that you're as drunk as they are?

LOCKYER: He means that we've come for the flag of the regiment. We'll not harm you.

SMITH: You've come for the flag?

SEDLEY: Oh, this is talking to a deaf man. I'll fetch it.

CHURCH: Shall I give you a leg up?

SMITH: Lockyer: what is this?

LOCKYER: Lawful mutiny.

SMITH: Mutiny? Bloody hell. They are drunk.

JOAN: No they're not.

SMITH: Of course they are. Come on, Lockyer. Go back to your billets. I'll forget what's been said.

LOCKYER: Right, lads. Up you go. Smash that door down.

LANDLORD: Oh no you don't!

CHURCH: Get out of the way.

LANDLORD: Smith - do what he wants. When soldiers smash things nobody pays for them.

SMITH: Lockyer. They punish mutiny by death.

SOLDIER ON GALLERY: If they don't want us to mutiny why don't they give us our pay?

LANDLORD: Don't wreck that door! I'll open it!

SMITH: Lockyer: Colonel Whalley's two minutes away, in Cheapside.

LOCKYER: Colonel Whalley's no longer in command.

[*Cheers and shouts of "Praise the Lord!" from soldiers on the galleries.*]

SMITH: Don't be ridiculous. Who is in command? Oh, no. Don't tell me. Captain William Thompson.

LOCKYER: He is: and freely elected.

SMITH: You've gone mad.

LOCKYER: Brother, give us the flag.

SMITH: You're as bad as those Diggers.

SEDLEY: Myself, I'm not absolutely against Diggers.

CHURCH: They don't wash. All they do is dig.

SMITH: All you want's your back pay.

JOAN: What's·wrong with that?

   [*More cheers.*]

SMITH: We must fight the Irish first.

LOCKYER: Hand over the flag!

SMITH: No.

SEDLEY: Where is it?

JOAN: Oh come on. I'll get it.

SMITH: You're supposed to be on my side!

JOAN: Well, I'm not, am I?

   [*JOAN goes in for the flag. SEDLEY's pistol is levelled at
   SMITH. SMITH looks round. He makes a final appeal.*]

SMITH: Corporal: soldiers: I order you to arrest Robert
   Lockyer!

   [*The drummer and musician start to play* Babylon is
   Fallen.]

LOCKYER: Brothers. You know me, your comrade,
   Robert Lockyer. Brothers, the time of deliverance is at
   hand!

[*One or two soldiers sing the first verse. Others join in the chorus.*]

Hail the day so long expected
Hail the day of long release
Zion's walls are now erected
And her watchmen publish peace
Throughout Shiloh's wide dominion
Hear the trumpet loudly roar.

CHORUS: Babylon is fallen, is fallen, is fallen
Babylon is fallen to rise no more
Babylon is fallen, is fallen, is fallen
Babylon is fallen to rise no more.

LOCKYER: Our officers promised a new franchise and a
new parliament. But what they did was to purge the
old parliament, kill the King, and take power unto
themselves. They imprisoned our Leveller brethren
and rejected our proposals. And now they say
"Invade the Irish" – and if we refuse they disband us
without pay.

[*This time the soldiers sing the verse but more join in the chorus.*]

All the merchants stand in wonder
What is this has come to pass?
Murmuring like a distant thunder
Crying "Oh, alas, alas!"
Swell the ranks, ye kings and nobles
Priests and people, rich and poor.

CHORUS: Babylon is fallen, is fallen, is fallen
Babylon is fallen to rise no more
Babylon is fallen, is fallen, is fallen
Babylon is fallen to rise no more.

LOCKYER: But we say, and we cry it aloud to the
people of London, we say that we do not seek to

disturb any man. We seek what is just, for ourselves, and for other nations. And that is why we ask – to what end should we engage our lives against the Irish? To make our officers as absolute masters over Ireland as we have made them over England? Or is the land and inheritance which any nation has enjoyed not their right, which God and nature have given them? What was the purpose in our wading in a stream of Christian blood? Did we overturn one tyranny to be enslaved by another? Brothers, join me and good men like William Thompson in this lawful mutiny!

[*By now JOAN has the flag over her shoulder and the soldiers and other women have come down from the galleries. The end of the song is triumphant.*]

Sound the trumpet on Mount Zion
Christ is come a second time
Ruling with a rod of iron
All who now as foes combine
Babel's garments we've rejected
And our fellowship is sure.

CHORUS: Babylon is fallen, is fallen, is fallen
Babylon is fallen to rise no more
Babylon is fallen, is fallen, is fallen
Babylon is fallen to rise no more...

[*LOCKYER at their head, and JOAN following with the flag, the mutineers march out of the inn. SMITH and the LANDLORD are left alone as the chorus fades down the street.*]

SMITH: She's gone with them! And what did you do? Nothing!

LANDLORD: Well: whoever wins, they'll still have to pay me for their ale, won't they?

SCENE THREE

DEBENTURES

May, 1649

An army post. LAWRENCE CLARKSON, a common soldier, has been asked to see CAPTAIN KIRBY. CLARKSON is about 30. He was born in Preston. KIRBY is not much older.

KIRBY: Clarkson. Is that you, Clarkson?

CLARKSON: Yes sir.

KIRBY: Did you write this pamphlet?

CLARKSON: Eh?

KIRBY: [*Reading.*] "Who are the oppressors but the nobility and the gentry, and who are the oppressed if not the yeoman, the farmer, the tradesman and the like? Have you not chosen oppressors to redeem you from oppression?"

CLARKSON: Of course we have.

KIRBY: [*Reading.*] "Your slavery is their liberty..."

CLARKSON: [*Picking up the quotation.*] "Your poverty is their prosperity..." You know damn well I wrote it. Two years ago.

KIRBY: I see you remember the fruity bits.

CLARKSON: Because they're brilliant. What's up?

KIRBY: Is it true you want to leave the army?

CLARKSON: The lads admire you, Captain. You do your duty and never meddle with conscience.

KIRBY: The very reason, Clarkson, why rumours come to me like wenches in the night: very often. Is it true?

CLARKSON: How come you want to know?

KIRBY: Because this regiment's on its way to Ireland, Clarkson, and your pamphlets have been re-read in London.

CLARKSON: Praise the Lord.

KIRBY: By important officers and divines who in a general way of speech might be called government snoopers.

CLARKSON: Eh?

KIRBY: They want to boot you out.

CLARKSON: Me, sir? Why sir?

KIRBY: There's enough trouble with mutiny as it is.

CLARKSON: Mutiny? My thoughts are of God's purpose on earth, sir.

KIRBY: Yes – and General Cromwell's purpose is that we conquer Ireland, sell the land and have money to pay the army's wages. But if they boot you out first you won't get paid at all, will you?

CLARKSON: I've not been given much anyway, have I, except in paper debentures?

KIRBY: Where are they?

CLARKSON: Oh Lord God, Thou showest me this man's drift.

KIRBY: Where are they?

CLARKSON: In my bandolier.

KIRBY: The Colonel said "Kirby," he said, "there are doubts raised by Clarkson's extremism. Wouldn't it be better if before I'm told to kick him out he went of his own accord and we paid him cash for his debentures?"

CLARKSON: How much?

KIRBY: Half face-value.

CLARKSON: Half?

KIRBY: In some regiments you'd get a quarter.

CLARKSON: What will you buy when you cash 'em all in?

KIRBY: Some of this cavalier property that's coming on the market. Or maybe part of Ireland.

CLARKSON: Brother: where were you born?

KIRBY: Huddersfield. Worked like a dog all my life.

CLARKSON: What at?

KIRBY: The clothing shears. What else? War broke out and I thought: get off your arse, lad. Here's your only chance.

[*They look at each other. CLARKSON is holding the pat slips. Then CLARKSON gives the slips to KIRBY, who flicks through them to check the value. Then KIRBY gives CLARKSON the money.*]

Count it.

CLARKSON: Eh?

KIRBY: Count it.

[*CLARKSON counts it.*]

CLARKSON: You were sure I'd accept, weren't you?

KIRBY: Sign.

[*CLARKSON signs it.*]

Thank you. That's you and the army put asunder.

CLARKSON: Thank you.

KIRBY: Where will you go?

CLARKSON: I have it upon me to be solitary, and walk alone in a wilderness condition...

KIRBY: I was afraid you might.

CLARKSON: I must bring forth the truth that is within me...

KIRBY: Truth? Within you?

CLARKSON: That ill becomes you, brother.

KIRBY: [*Wanting to end the conversation.*] Thank you, Clarkson.

CLARKSON: The man at the clothing-shears would not have said that.

KIRBY: I've worked harder than you ever did.

CLARKSON: Not what I'm talking about.

KIRBY: Eh?

CLARKSON: Look at this. Eh? Eh? What am I doing, eh? Eh?

KIRBY: Clenching your fist.

CLARKSON: No! No! Don't you understand? Don't you understand what I'm doing?

[*CLARKSON is holding out both arms and clenching his fists. He shakes with the effort. Then he stamps and shouts once or twice. He almost whistles. Then he stops. The effort has left him drained as well as fiercely perplexed. He breathes deeply.*]

But it will come out, brother. Truth must come out.

[*As KIRBY watches CLARKSON go, voices sing.*]

He who would valiant be
'gainst all disaster
Let him in constancy
Follow the Master
There's no discouragement
Shall make him once relent
His first avowed intent
To be a pilgrim...

SCENE FOUR

BURFORD
May 14, 1649

A soldier named SYNDERCOMBE stands sentry in a meadow outside the little town. It is dusk. EVERARD approaches, shouting and waving his arms.

EVERARD: Hey! Hey! Is this Burford?

SYNDERCOMBE: Don't move!

EVERARD: Don't threaten me, lad. I've been in more mutinies than you've had hot dinners.

SYNDERCOMBE: Who are you?

EVERARD: Everard.

SYNDERCOMBE: Eh?

EVERARD: I'm the famous Everard.

SYNDERCOMBE: Never heard of you.

EVERARD: Call William Thompson.

SYNDERCOMBE: Captain Thompson! [*To EVERARD.*] Don't move! [*Calling again.*] Captain Thompson!

EVERARD: I've had these headaches. Truth dazzles me. It gives me headaches.

[*SYNDERCOMBE watches him.*]

I've known the power of apparitions, and been the vessel of Israel's wrath. What's your regiment?

SYNDERCOMBE: Whalley's Dragoons.

EVERARD: Were you in the London mutiny?

SYNDERCOMBE: Yes.

EVERARD: Did you see Robert Lockyer executed?

SYNDERCOMBE: Yes.

EVERARD: How did he die?

SYNDERCOMBE: He just stood there and looked at them.

EVERARD: Aye. Word came. Is not Cromwell Nebuchadnezzar? Yet here's truth working. By sending your regiment to Banbury he spread the word himself. Nebuchadnezzar spread mutiny himself! I see waterfalls! Blinding waterfalls!

[*CAPTAIN THOMPSON arrives. He sees EVERARD shielding his eyes as from a blinding light, and SYNDERCOMBE staring at him.*]

THOMPSON: Soldier. Your mouth's dropped open in dismay.

SYNDERCOMBE: It's this man, sir. I think he might be convulsed.

THOMPSON: Aye. He is. Convulsed with the woes and hopes of Israel.

[*EVERARD unshields his eyes.*]

EVERARD: William? William Thompson?

[*EVERARD sees THOMPSON. They embrace.*]

Here. I have a letter from Winstanley.

[*They embrace again.*]

Yea, Lord, are not this man's soldiers risen in lawful mutiny Israel's sure hope and shield!

THOMPSON: I've got eight regiments. And my brother. And Henry Dean. And old Mr Eyres. Can you imagine? Eight regiments!

[*They laugh and embrace again.*]

How's Winstanley? Was he annoyed to see you leave?

EVERARD: He's never annoyed is he? He's a bleeding saint.

THOMPSON: Is the soil there good or bad?

EVERARD: I met Fairfax. He despised me. He knew I saw through him. He won't be shown the promised opportunity. What's obvious now is that the opportunity will be revealed to Cromwell.

THOMPSON: There was a skirmish today.

EVERARD: Who with?

THOMPSON: Our cavalry and their covering regiments.

EVERARD: Babylonians!

THOMPSON: We made them keep their distance.

EVERARD: Have you seen Cromwell yet?

THOMPSON: No. I've met his emissary.

EVERARD: Who's that?

THOMPSON: Major White.

EVERARD: I don't know him.

THOMPSON: He's straight enough.

EVERARD: What does he say?

THOMPSON: He says that our demands are reasonable.

EVERARD: All of them?

THOMPSON: All of them. We're to meet tomorrow.

EVERARD: You and White?

THOMPSON: Me and Cromwell.

EVERARD: Yea Lord!

[*EVERARD is so excited that he paces about THOMPSON watches him, smiling. Then EVERARD stops.*]

The opportunity will be revealed to Cromwell!

THOMPSON: What upsets me is that so many good lads had to die to make it happen.

EVERARD: Aye: but think of it: they'll have their revenge in fields of asphodel.

SCENE FIVE

MRS ASHLEY'S
May 14, 1649

Later.

[*Several of Whalley's Dragoons, including SEDLEY and SYNDERCOMBE, who is fast asleep, are billeted in the cottage of a widow named MRS ASHLEY. JOAN is with them. MRS ASHLEY peers out of the window. One soldier quietly sings.*]

Will you come to the rolling of the stone

The tossing of the ball
And will you come and see pretty Suzie
Dance among you all
Will you drink of the blood
The white and the red
And will you come and see pretty Suzie
When that I am dead
Suzie charms the birds from the sky
The fish from out the bay
And there she lay in her true lover's arms
And there she's contented to stay.

[*MRS ASHLEY scurries back to her place and pretends to be asleep. CORPORAL CHURCH enters. He settles down, using his saddle as a pillow. Then he realises that MRS ASHLEY is faking.*]

CHURCH: Did you watch out of the window while I was having a piss?

[*Silence.*]

I said: did you watch me having a piss?

SEDLEY: Shut up.

CHURCH: She watched me.

SEDLEY: Who cares?

[*Silence. Then CHURCH goes to MRS ASHLEY and whispers fiercely.*]

CHURCH: I know you're not bloody asleep.

[*MRS ASHLEY retorts.*]

MRS ASHLEY: Irish? Irish? Pigs. That's what the Irish are.

CHURCH: Who's talking about the Irish?

MRS ASHLEY: You are: and it's disgusting.

CHURCH: Why did you watch me having a piss?

MRS ASHLEY: Because I don't trust you, that's why.

CHURCH: Woman, you've nothing worth stealing.

MRS ASHLEY: I've six wonderful hens.

CHURCH: Then sleep in the coop.

MRS ASHLEY: I've worked hard since my husband died. Hard work. I know what hard work is.

CHURCH: Are you the householder?

MRS ASHLEY: Of course I am.

SEDLEY: Why can't you two shut up?

CHURCH: Sedley: tomorrow morning Cromwell will agree to our terms. Won't he?

SEDLEY: Oh, Jesus... Yes.

CHURCH: Do you realise that if this woman was a man she would then have the vote?

SEDLEY: But she's not a man, is she?

CHURCH: It's bloody frightening, that's what it is.

MRS ASHLEY: Oh, I'm going to complain to your officer.

SEDLEY: That's no use, love. We elected him.

CHURCH: It should be more than just servants and paupers that don't get the vote: there should be reading and writing and stupidity tests.

SEDLEY: How well can you read?

CHURCH: What's that got to do with it?

SEDLEY: You're not a householder, either.

[*Stalemate.*]

CHURCH: Some people have no idea what they're fighting for, nor of simple justice.

[*Silence. They settle down. Out of the silence, JOAN sings softly to the dozing SEDLEY.*]

Fly up my cock
You're my well-feathered cock
And don't crow till the break of day
And your red rosy comb shall be of beaten gold
And your neck of silvery grey
My cock he flew up and my cock he flew down
But he crowed one hour too soon
This young man arose and he hurried on his clothes
But it was only the light of the moon
When will you come back my dear Jimmy she said
For to wed with a gay gold ring
Seven moons said he, shining over the sea
And the sky to yield up no more rain
For now I do see the contrary way
A man's forced to live single or be bound.

[*Silence. All is peaceful. Then suddenly SYNDERCOMBE wakes up with a cry.*]

SYNDERCOMBE: Ah... Ah... Where am I?

[*The others are woken, too.*]

MRS ASHLEY: What's your name, lad?

SYNDERCOMBE: Myles Syndercombe.

MRS ASHLEY: How old are you?

SYNDERCOMBE: Seventeen.

MRS ASHLEY: Have you got a young woman?

SYNDERCOMBE: What if I have?

CHURCH: He hasn't, has he?

SYNDERCOMBE: Yes I have.

MRS ASHLEY: Go back to her.

SYNDERCOMBE: I can't.

MRS ASHLEY: Set your mind to it.

SYNDERCOMBE: John the Baptist came to me at night.
    He said: remember, there's Irish lasses with men at
    the war.

   [*Silence.*]

SEDLEY: There's lasses everywhere, Steepleboom.

SYNDERCOMBE: Syndercombe.

CHURCH: Fortunately, I'm not married to any of 'em.

MRS ASHLEY: You filthy sod.

CHURCH: You get stuffed.

   [*Silence. Everybody settles down and seems to be going to
   sleep.*]

SYNDERCOMBE: Corporal...

   [*No reply.*]

Cromwell and Fairfax did promise not to march
against us, didn't they? They did say our demands
were just?

   [*No reply.*]

Well, in their hearts everybody hates war and so on,
don't they?

   [*A pointed snore from SEDLEY. SYNDERCOMBE seems
   to take a hint but he cannot resist another question.*]

Will we see him tomorrow?

[*CHURCH gets up on his elbow and glares at SYNDERCOMBE.*]

CHURCH: What?

SYNDERCOMBE: Cromwell...

CHURCH: Go to sleep.

[*CHURCH settles down.*]

SYNDERCOMBE: If we do see him how will I know him?

CHURCH: Nose.

SYNDERCOMBE: Eh?

CHURCH: He has a very red nose.

SYNDERCOMBE: Oh...

[*Even SYNDERCOMBE settles.*]

Nobody in our parish has seen him. Nobody.

[*Silence. Then sleep. Then noise. A trumpet. Shouts of command. Musketry. CHURCH wakes up.*]

CHURCH: Soldier!

[*The noise is much nearer. The others wake up.*]

It's Cromwell. It's bloody blasted Cromwell.

SEDLEY: What?

CHURCH: He's attacked us.

MRS ASHLEY: Help me. Help me. I must hide my pewter spoons.

SEDLEY: What's she talking about?

CHURCH: She's a daft bitch.

SYNDERCOMBE: What's happening?

CHURCH: Run!

[*CHURCH leads the rush to the door but it is too late. CROMWELL and his soldiers are already there. Momentary silence.*]

Well. There you are, Steepleboom. You've seen him.

SYNDERCOMBE: Eh?

CHURCH: Cromwell.

CROMWELL: Take these deluded men away.

[*Soldiers hustle them.*]

SYNDERCOMBE: You kept not covenant with us. You kept not covenant.

CROMWELL: Nor you with God, soldier.

[*They are taken out.*]

Nor you with God.

SCENE SIX

CROMWELL'S SALVATION
May 15, 1649

The early hours of the morning and not yet light.

[*CROMWELL has set up his command post in The Bull Inn. In 1649 he was fifty years old, which was much older in that epoch than it would be today. He was a modest country gentleman whose life seemed to have run its course when the Civil War changed everything. FAIRFAX arrives, wrapped in his cloak.*]

FAIRFAX: By God: Oxfordshire. I thought we had all the cold mornings up North. What's the reckoning?

CROMWELL: One mutineer killed. Three hundred and fifty men and six hundred horses captured. About nine hundred men ran away, Captain Thompson among them.

FAIRFAX: What about his brother?

CROMWELL: We caught him: and our old friend Mr Eyres: and Cornet Dean. Mr Eyres is too old and too silly and too well-connected.

FAIRFAX: Aye.

CROMWELL: We should shoot Thompson, Dean, and two Corporals: Church and Perkins.

FAIRFAX: We can't shoot Dean.

CROMWELL: God will find a way.

[*Drumbeats. CORNET THOMPSON, CORPORAL CHURCH and CORPORAL PERKINS are marched in.*]

FAIRFAX: Lads. What came over you, lads?

CHURCH: Liberty, general. Have you heard of it?

FAIRFAX: I have, and I wish I'd not meddled with it.

CHURCH: That's rich.

FAIRFAX: I've more on my conscience than you know exists. This is a drumhead court martial, and you're sentenced to death.

[*PERKINS almost buckles against CHURCH.*]

CHURCH: I don't want your weight.

CROMWELL: You'll be shot at daybreak against the churchyard wall. Amen.

[*The three men are marched out to drumbeats.*]

FAIRFAX: That remark about my conscience was heartfelt, Oliver.

CROMWELL: You've surely no qualms about mutineers.

FAIRFAX: No. But I had about the King. I felt sick at that. And I feel sick at Ireland.

CROMWELL: Will you strike sail before the ship reaches port?

FAIRFAX: I feel even worse when I realise that after Ireland you must invade Scotland. Oh, I know it's necessary. The Commonwealth must be safe, and kind words will not do with cavaliers. But to me it comes hard. It's not natural, as self-defence is. So I'll resign.

[*Silence.*]

Oh, don't worry. I'll stand by you till next year.

CROMWELL: I'd sooner serve under you than command the finest army in Europe.

FAIRFAX: You do command it, Oliver. I have the title Lord General to appease the men of money.

CROMWELL: I respect you too much to dispute it.

FAIRFAX: Well, I've never respected this Henry Dean. Let's be done with him. Sergeant!

[*Drumbeats. HENRY DEAN is marched in.*]

Dean. By drumhead court martial you've been found guilty of mutiny and sentenced to death.

DEAN: Traitors!

CROMWELL: Hold your tongue! You'll be shot at daybreak against the churchyard wall. Amen.

DEAN: You can't shoot me. I was your man. I let you into Burford. I told you where the sentries were posted. I –

[*FAIRFAX slaps him across the face. DEAN is shocked into silence.*]

CROMWELL: Dean. The Lord will find a way. My chaplain will visit you. Do you understand?

[*DEAN is marched out to drumbeats. There is a little silence.*]

Do you know why Dean betrayed his friends?

FAIRFAX: Why?

CROMWELL: He wanted you and me murdered. When his friends refused he despaired, and betrayed them. Sergeant!

[*Drumbeat. MR EYRES is marched in. He is about seventy years old and a member of the minor gentry. He did not have time to dress and is wrapped in a blanket. He tries to look like a soldier, but is shaken.*]

Well. Mr Eyres. My very old friend.

EYRES: It's not well at all. It's ill.

CROMWELL: To be caught with your breeches off?

EYRES: Oliver Cromwell, I've known you all your life. I saw your mother send a maid into the street to tan your backside. I saw that happen, fifty years ago.

CROMWELL: Were you as silly then as you are now?

EYRES: Don't you dare speak to me like that. I was with you before the war when you helped poor people thrown off their land. I joined the first troop of cavalry you ever raised. Now look at you. Call a parliament!

CROMWELL: Would you invade Ireland?

EYRES: Never.

CROMWELL: Oh. Then you'll submit to the young Stuart's Irish army?

EYRES: What I will do is speak for England.

CROMWELL: England? You had twelve hundred men here out of an army of fifty thousand.

FAIRFAX: Poor people, deluded by some cunning and turbulent spirits.

EYRES: Once you were turbulent.

CROMWELL: Your levelling principle would make the tenant as liberal a fortune as the landlord. A pleasing voice to all poor men, and truly not unwelcome to bad men. Therefore we brought the mutinous regiments together so that we could crush them together.

EYRES: I'll not believe you. Traitor!

CROMWELL: As for your reproaches, leaves do not stay on the trees for ever, nor do the trees stay bare for ever. God's will endures but we die daily and must be born again daily. I shall send you to Oxford jail, old friend, where the lawyers will find it difficult to hold you.

EYRES: Oxford jail?

CROMWELL: You'll be back home in a month: for what charges can we bring?

EYRES: I've led these men, haven't I?

FAIRFAX: Mr Eyres, you're no longer a soldier, so you can't be a mutineer, can you?

EYRES: I'm guilty of sedition. I – Oliver, you've no right to ignore me.

[*CROMWELL and FAIRFAX exchange glances.*]

How dare you laugh at me!

FAIRFAX: Mr Eyres: when the army's paid and God gives us a good harvest, these tumults will die down.

EYRES: There are men all over England with new fires in their blood.

CROMWELL: Your blanket's slipping. Take him out.

[*MR EYRES is marched out to drumbeats.*]

FAIRFAX: I want the prisoners on the church roof to witness execution.

[*CROMWELL nods. It will be done.*]

Now – I won't sleep, but I can lie down for an hour or two.

[*FAIRFAX goes. CROMWELL is alone. He prays.*]

CROMWELL: Lord. Lord God, I know that it is You who tells me what to do. One day when I was young, You told me that I was saved. I felt a restlessness that mastered me the more I tried to master it. In the fingers. The upper arm. Shoulders. Jaw. Rictus. I knew real hell and then transfigured dizziness. I walked but could not feel the earth, and what was this, O Lord, if not a state of Grace? Your breath in my body. Your love and my knowledge of salvation. Since then I have always obeyed Your messages in my body. Headaches of unease. Conscience, like a string drawn through the bowels. These are my assurances from a purpose that I no longer even seek to understand, but only to obey, in the sure faith that it is good. I know that what I do here is good. I know that what I will do in Ireland is good, because my body sings with ease. For all this world, and all these foolish men, all this is dung and dross beside the face of Christ!

SCENE SEVEN

BURFORD CHURCHYARD
May 15, 1649

Daybreak.

[*The prisoners and their women and the people of the village watch, and so do CROMWELL and FAIRFAX, as the firing squad march to their position.*]

MUSKETEER OFFICER: Musketeers. Forward march.

[*The line is in place.*]

Halt. Face to your right. Stand right in your ranks. Silence. To your General charge your musket.

[*The musketeers make their bow to FAIRFAX, who acknowledges. Drumbeat. CHURCH, PERKINS and THOMPSON are marched out.*]

Advance your musket. Order your musket. Give your rest to your musket. Open your pan. Clear your pan. Prime your pan. Shut your pan.

[*Led by the women, the prisoners sing. The musket drill continues.*]

Bright morning star arising
Bright morning star arising
Bright morning star arising
Day is a-breaking in my soul.

Cast off your loose powder. Blow off your loose powder. Cast about your musket and trail your rest. Open your charge. Charge with powder. Charge with bullet. Draw forth your scouring stick. Shorten your scouring stick. Ram home.

O where are our dear brothers
O where are our dear brothers
O where are our dear brothers
Day is a-breaking in my soul.

Withdraw your scouring stick. Shorten your scouring stick. Return your scouring stick. Poise your musket and recover your rest. Give your rest to your musket. Wind your lock. Open your pan. Present upon your rest. Give fire breast high.

[*The preparations and the singing stop together.*]

CHURCH: Brothers. Shoot me when I hold out my hands to you.

[*CHURCH holds out his hands.*]

MUSKETEER OFFICER: Fire!

[*The volley crashes out. CHURCH, PERKINS and THOMPSON are killed. The singing begins again. DEAN is marched out. The OFFICER takes up the orders again.*]

They are in the valley praying
They are in the valley praying
They are in the valley praying
Day is a-breaking in my soul.

MUSKETEER OFFICER: Dismount your musket and order. Give your rest to your musket. Clear your pan. Prime your pan. Shut your pan. Cast off your loose powder.

DEAN: Lord God. Lord. I see him. There. Among the willows. In the long grass.

MUSKETEER OFFICER: Silence.

DEAN: I see the Lord Jesus walking in Burford. I am saved. I know that I am saved.

CROMWELL: Amen. Release that man. It is not God's will that he should die today.

MUSKETEER OFFICER: Draw forth your files.

VOICES: Alleluia! Alleluia brother!

CROMWELL: God's will is that the Commonwealth should be secure.

[*The singing starts again.*]

Some are gone to heaven shouting
Some are gone to heaven shouting
Some are gone to heaven shouting
Day is a-breaking in my soul
Bright morning star arising
Bright morning star arising
Bright morning star arising
Day is a-breaking in my soul.

INTERVAL

SCENE EIGHT

BRADFIELD RECTORY
Summer, 1649

Bradfield Rectory is the very rich living of the REVEREND JOHN PORDAGE, son of a London merchant, graduate of All Souls, Oxford, and a well-to-do believer in left-wing ideas. EVERARD appears. He is travel-weary, emotional, and glad to have found his haven.

EVERARD: Mr Pordage! Mr Pordage! Who's there? Mr Pordage!

[*LUCY, a servant-girl, pops up from behind a hedge. She is semi-clad.*]

LUCY: Oh...!

EVERARD: I must see Mr Pordage.

LUCY: Oh dear...

[*LUCY runs giggling into the house.*]

EVERARD: Hey. Come here. What's happening?

[*A very dishevelled MR PORDAGE now pops his head up from behind the hedge.*]

PORDAGE: What d'you want? Who is it?

EVERARD: Mr Pordage?

PORDAGE: It's not you, Everard?

EVERARD: I need help, sir. I need it bad.

PORDAGE: I say, I'm awfully sorry about this, I was – I mean I was just – well, as you know, I don't believe in the enslavements of matrimony.

EVERARD: I was at Burford when Cromwell smashed the mutiny.

PORDAGE: They found William Thompson and killed him. Did you know?

EVERARD: Yes.

PORDAGE: But you escaped?

EVERARD: To London. Where I was not safe with this mood upon me.

PORDAGE: Good heavens. I say, I'm awfully glad to see you. You must stay as long as you like. I've had a revelation that there's not one spiritual world but two, extending and penetrating through the whole visible creation...

[*ABIEZER COPPE arrives. He is 30 years old and another well-to-do radical. He came from Warwick, met PORDAGE at Oxford, and has been preacher to an army garrison.*]

COPPE: Look here, Pordage, what's wrong with the maid Lucy? She's squeaking like a little mouse.

PORDAGE: This is William Everard. He discovered Lucy and I when we were – I mean, we were in the clover, as the common folk say, and – This is Abiezer Coppe, a fellow student of mine at Oxford, and of late an army chaplain.

COPPE: Everard? Everard? By God, sir, but I've read your pamphlets.

EVERARD: The power has come back to me.

PORDAGE: Power? What power?

EVERARD: I have the power to raise up the dragon.

[*EVERARD raises up the dragon.*]

Alacamanza! Alacamanza! Behold! Smell the stink of his sulphur!

PORDAGE: He's spouting fire at me!

COPPE: He's jumping through the trees!

[*The dragon vanishes.*]

EVERARD: Sometimes the power leaves me. Sometimes I am at peace upon the bosom of the ocean.

[*There is a vision of angels and sweet music.*]

PORDAGE: Coppe. Coppe. He's conjured up angels.

COPPE: What music!

PORDAGE: What blessed harmony!

COPPE: I smell roses.

EVERARD: I smell the honeysuckle.

PORDAGE: Yes, truly, the harvest will be bountiful...

[*The angels disappear.*]

EVERARD: Where are they? Where have they gone?

PORDAGE: I knew it. There are two spiritual realities.

EVERARD: And one of them is the giant! Alacamanza! Alacamanza!

[*The giant appears.*]

PORDAGE: Ah! Ah!

COPPE: There is a sword in his hand.

PORDAGE: What loathsome hellish tastes!

EVERARD: Begone!

[*The giant disappears.*]

I do not want this power. Thompson is dead. Yea, the Jews are dispersed. I see blinding lights. Oh, Jesus, wrap me in honeysuckle...

PORDAGE: I never thought, when I came to this rectory, to see such sights within its garden.

[*LUCY appears, squealing more than before.*]

LUCY: Oh... Oh... Oh... Oh!

PORDAGE: What's the matter now, Lucy?

LUCY: I'm being chased by a dragon.

PORDAGE: No you aren't.

COPPE: By God, John, but she is.

[*The dragon appears again.*]

EVERARD: Its breath's on fire!

PORDAGE: Look out!

LUCY: Ah!

COPPE: Oh sulphurous hell!

[*LUCY screams and PORDAGE dances up and down.*]

PORDAGE: Not at my feet! Don't shoot flames at my feet!

[*Everyone coughs and splutters.*]

EVERARD: Begone! For Christ's sake leave my brain!

[*The dragon disappears. There is a relieved silence.*]

PORDAGE: I swear that during your stay, Mr Everard, I will keep to the virgin life.

LUCY: You'll what?

PORDAGE: I do not want you to be chased by a dragon, nor my stockings to be scorched.

[*LUCY bursts into tears.*]

Oh, Lucy!

LUCY: What about Tom Webster? Can I still do it with him?

PORDAGE: I don't know. Can she?

EVERARD: Nay, I know not. For I know not what these revelations mean.

LUCY: Well, how soon d'you reckon on finding out?

COPPE: What these revelations mean is that honour, nobility, gentility, property and superfluity have been the fruit of hellish horrid pride. Yea, the cause of all the blood that hath ever been shed, from the blood of the righteous Abel to the blood of the last Levellers that were shot to death.

PORDAGE: Yea: but what is the future?

COPPE: We disavow both sword-levelling and digging-levelling.

EVERARD: You can't. It must be one or the other.

COPPE: What frighted you? The very shadow of levelling: sword-levelling: man-levelling frighted you (and who can blame you, because it shook your kingdom) but now the substantiality of Levelling is coming.

PORDAGE: Thus saith the Lord God.

COPPE: Remove the diadem and take off the crown. Exalt him that is low and abuse him that is high. I will overturn, overturn, overturn it, and it shall be no more until he comes whose right it is.

LUCY: Yes. But can I do it with Tom Webster?

PORDAGE: Actually, I don't think so.

LUCY: Why not?

PORDAGE: There's a pillar of flame coming through the wheatfield.

COPPE: Good Lord.

PORDAGE: Make for the house!

EVERARD: Alacamanza! Leave me! Leave me!

[*They run off, pursued by a pillar of flame.*]

SCENE NINE

ARMY HEADQUARTERS
Summer, 1649

WINSTANLEY has again been summoned to meet FAIRFAX and his officers, this time at Army Headquarters near Walton-on-Thames.

FAIRFAX: Mr Winstanley: I have once again been asked by the Council of State to enquire into these disturbances.

WINSTANLEY: We have caused no disturbance.

FAIRFAX: I think you have.

WINSTANLEY: A band of men from Walton destroyed our barley crop.

FAIRFAX: Did you admonish them?

WINSTANLEY: We did. For which Parson Platt had six

of our men arrested. They were brought to Walton where they were held prisoner in the church and abused and insulted.

FAIRFAX: They were released by a Justice of the Peace.

[*Silence.*]

Now, on what grounds did he release them?

WINSTANLEY: An officer of the law was not present at the riot which they were said to have caused.

[*FAIRFAX nods.*]

Whereupon John Turnbull led a mob of two hundred persons who stole our spades and tools and again threw our men into prison.

FAIRFAX: From which they were again released, and Mr Turnbull was ordered to return the tools.

WINSTANLEY: Which he has not done.

FAIRFAX: Ah. Yet the law seems to have protected you.

WINSTANLEY: No. We live in fear and danger.

FAIRFAX: What do you expect if you trespass?

WINSTANLEY: We do not trespass.

FAIRFAX: You trespass against the Lord of the Manor.

WINSTANLEY: The land we dig belonged to the tyrant Stuart.

FAIRFAX: It was passed to the Lord of the Manor.

WINSTANLEY: The death of the tyrant has confounded all such claims.

FAIRFAX: Is not true liberty knowing, by a certain law, that our wives, our children, our servants and our goods are most our own?

WINSTANLEY: True liberty lies in the community of spirit, and community in the earthly treasury. When once the earth becomes a common treasury, the enmity of all lands will cease, and none shall dare to seek dominion over others, neither shall any dare to kill one another, nor desire more of the earth than another.

FAIRFAX: Mr Winstanley: your beliefs will destroy all our government, and all our ministry and religion.

WINSTANLEY: It is very true. Freedom is the man that will turn the world upside down: therefore no wonder he hath enemies.

FAIRFAX: Against whom, I think, you seek my protection.

[*Silence.*]

I say that the law is your protection.

WINSTANLEY: Law is but the declarative will of conquerors, how they will have their subjects to be ruled.

FAIRFAX: I urge you once again to keep the peace, and to place your trust in the law: as I have tried to do all my life.

SCENE TEN

THE ROAD TO LONDON
September 30, 1649

ABIEZER COPPE is walking to London. He meets upon the way a BEGGAR, a most strange, deformed man clad in patched clouts. COPPE passes the BEGGAR and then stops.

COPPE: Is it my heart, or the day of the Lord, which burns as an oven in me?

[*COPPE turns to the beggar.*]

How now, friend. Are you poor?

BEGGAR: Yes, master. Very poor.

[*COPPE starts to tremble. He has to embrace himself to hold himself still.*]

COPPE: Are you poor?

BEGGAR: Yea, very poor.

COPPE: It's a poor wretch. Give him two pence.

[*COPPE turns his back on the BEGGAR.*]

Nay. It's a poor wretch. Give him sixpence. That's enough for a squire or a knight to give one poor body. Besides, he is worse than an infidel that provides not for his own family. True love begins at home. Me and my family are fed, as the young ravens, strangely. I have been a preacher and I have abhorred both tithes and hire. I don't know who will give me the worth of a penny. Have a care of the main chance.

[*COPPE pulls out a coin.*]

Give me sixpence, here's a shilling for you.

BEGGAR: I cannot. I have never a penny.

COPPE: I would fain have given you something, if you could have changed my money.

BEGGAR: God bless you.

[*COPPE walks away.*]

COPPE: Ah! Ah! The rust of my silver consumes my flesh as with fire.

[*COPPE turns back and gives the man money then he walks away again.*]

I will continue joyfully to London, for I feel the sparkles of a great glory arising up from under these ashes.

[*Again COPPE checks. He takes off his hat and bows to the man, seven times.*]

Because I am a King I have done this. But you need not tell anyone.

SCENE ELEVEN

GOLDSMITHS HALL
October, 1649

COPPE arrives in Foster Lane outside Goldsmiths Hall, London. He paces back and forth in a state of high concentration. Men of business pass to and fro, some with their wives. CAPTAIN KIRBY, whom he last saw in his army post, arrives. He is not sure of the way. He asks COPPE.

KIRBY: Good day, sir. I'm in the army, as you see, and newly arrived from Ireland. I don't know London very well. This is the Goldsmiths Hall, right?

COPPE: It is, sir.

KIRBY: Thank you.

COPPE: This is the Goldsmiths Hall, from where Parliament directs the confiscation and resale of Cavalier lands.

KIRBY: Thank you.

[*KIRBY starts to walk away. COPPE checks him.*]

COPPE: From Ireland, you said?

KIRBY: Yes.

[*Again KIRBY walks on. Again COPPE checks him.*]

COPPE: Ah! You are a conqueror!

KIRBY: Thank you for your directions. Good day.

COPPE: You have come to London, sir, unless I am
mistaken about the world of usury, which I am not
because my father was a part of it, to double up on
your investment!

KIRBY: Sir, if you're some kind of broker, I must warn
you that I'm to meet my own advisors in the Hall.

COPPE: My advice, sir, is that I am God. I made all
things in this world, and I say, deliver my money to
rogues, thieves, whores and cut-purses who are flesh
of thy flesh and every whit as good as thyself in mine
eye.

[*KIRBY stiffens. He deliberately does not look at COPPE.
COPPE shouts at point-blank range in an attempt to force
him to look.*]

The day of the Lord! The day of the Lord! The day of
the Lord!

[*COPPE howls and gnashes his teeth. He turns a cartwheel.*]

Have all things common or the plague of God will
rot and consume all you have! Howl! Howl ye noble,
howl honourable, howl ye rich men for the miseries
that are coming upon you! My hand is stretched still!
Your gold and silver is cankered! Do you not see my
hand stretched out?

[*People ignore COPPE.*]

It is a joy to Nehemiah to smite them and pluck off
their hair!

[*COPPE snatches hats and wigs and runs away, shouting.*]

The day of the Lord! The day of the Lord!

BYSTANDERS: Stop him! Stop thief! Stop thief!

KIRBY: The government must act against such madmen
as it acted against Ireland – otherwise a man could
work all his life and see no value in his land and
goods.

SCENE TWELVE

A VOTE TAKEN

October, 1649

*A raw afternoon. The DIGGERS are wrapped up as well
as they can be. They carry in RICHARD MAIDLEY, who
has been attacked and is bleeding about the head. They lay
him down to clean his wounds. There are WINSTANLEY,
MRS MAIDLEY, STEWER, COLTON and their wives,
JOHN TAYLOR and various others including a simple-
minded YOUNG WOMAN.*

MRS COLTON: Put him down here.

MRS STEWER: Who hit him?

COLTON: Soldiers.

MRS STEWER: Oh, no!

TAYLOR: Oh, yes. They stood in our way while we
worked and I said: ignore them; bloody ignore them.
But no, no. Mrs Colton argued and one of them
shoved her and Maidley shoved him back and that's
how it started.

MRS MAIDLEY ... [*Weeping.*] ...!

MRS COLTON: Oh, shut up, Mrs Maidley, love.

MRS MAIDLEY: He's my man.

MRS COLTON: Well if he's dead he's dead, and if he isn't we'll put some herbs on it.

MRS MAIDLEY: Richard. Richard...

MAIDLEY: Eh?

MRS MAIDLEY ... [*Weeping.*] ...!

WINSTANLEY: Hush, Mrs Maidley.

[*MAIDLEY groans. He is more aware.*]

COLTON: Maidley: how are you?

MAIDLEY: They were big men.

MRS COLTON: Don't move.

MAIDLEY: Ah..!

MRS COLTON: I said don't move.

MAIDLEY: I did hit one of them.

MRS MAIDLEY ... [*Weeping.*] ...!

[*TAYLOR has a stick. He relieves his feelings by banging it on the ground. Then he accuses COLTON.*]

TAYLOR: Just tell your wife it was her fault. Tell her to do what she's told.

COLTON: I've done my best. That's all I know.

STEWER: [*A bit old and daft.*] What? What does he say?

MRS STEWER: Nothing.

MRS COLTON: Not what I'd call nothing.

TAYLOR: You all know what I mean.

[*He bangs with his piece of wood.*]

WINSTANLEY: Brothers. Sisters. They've pulled down our buildings and attacked us with soldiers.

MRS STEWER: Which Fairfax promised they wouldn't.

TAYLOR: Fairfax is a Babylonian.

WINSTANLEY: Can we stay here longer?

STEWER: Cobham people are better than Walton people and always have been. I lived in Cobham all my life. Why didn't we dig in Cobham in the first place?

COLTON: Everard.

STEWER: Eh?

MRS STEWER: Everard said dig here.

TAYLOR: Aye, and where is he now? Run off when it became hard work.

WINSTANLEY: Nay, he's a good man and a true Leveller. He took me into his house.

MRS COLTON: He would. You did his thinking for him.

WINSTANLEY: They were his cows I minded – and saw die hard in winter.

STEWER: I still say why don't we dig in Cobham?

COLTON: You've said it every day for six months.

STEWER: Eh?

MRS STEWER: Nothing.

WINSTANLEY: Aye: for the common there is common. There is not even the shaving of an excuse for a landlord, as there is here. In Cobham we might await the opportunity in safety.

[*Silence.*]

Colton? Taylor? What do you say?

COLTON: It's winter coming, isn't it?

WINSTANLEY: Where else have we to go?

STEWER: Ask where they come from? Where did you all come from?

TAYLOR: I was like you, Stewer, on poor relief from Cobham parish.

[*STEWER points round the group.*]

SIMPLE-MIND: I lived in the forest. I ate hedgehogs.

COLTON: London.

MRS COLTON: We had money.

COLTON: They all know.

TAYLOR: He sawed wood in the dockyard. And we know why he left.

MRS COLTON: Hah!

COLTON: Oh, leave it, woman!

TAYLOR: He was caught stealing and whipped.

[*Silence.*]

MRS STEWER: Did I tell you? I dropped three leaves in a puddle this morning, and they all turned round the same way.

[*Silence.*]

Don't you know what it means?

COLTON: No.

MRS STEWER: It means a good harvest.

TAYLOR: No it doesn't.

MRS STEWER: It does.

MRS COLTON: Well the last one was hopeless wasn't it?

[*Silence.*]

WINSTANLEY: So if some stay here until we have at least one shelter built at Cobham – is that best? Maidley?

[*No reply.*]

Mrs Maidley?

MRS MAIDLEY: Richard speaks for us. Yes, then. We'll go.

WINSTANLEY: Colton?

COLTON: Aye.

[*WINSTANLEY looks at STEWER.*]

STEWER: Eh?

MRS STEWER: Aye.

WINSTANLEY: Fellow creature?

[*SIMPLE-MIND grins and agrees.*]

Taylor?

TAYLOR: No. I'll take my chance on the road.

WINSTANLEY: Do you want a share of the seed corn?

COLTON: That's not just.

WINSTANLEY: Yes it is.

TAYLOR: I don't want any.

[*As the camp breaks up the women sing a hymn that carries over WINSTANLEY's speech and the beginning of the next scene.*]

Repent repent ye sinners all
Repent now whilst ye may
For there's no repentance to be had
When our bodies are taken away.

WINSTANLEY: How easily it was done. But we have always known that when we have all in common we see Christ in other creatures as well as ourselves. So what need have we of imprisonment, whipping or hanging laws to bring one another into bondage?

SCENE THIRTEEN

WET WASHING
November, 1649

A bright, crisp day on the common land near the Digger camp at Cobham. MRS STEWER, MRS MAIDLEY, MRS COLTON and others are singing as they do their washing. LAWRENCE CLARKSON approaches. He has a pack on his back. He slips off the pack and watches the women. They giggle a bit but the song continues. CLARKSON walks round the women. He inspects each one. Choosing.

WOMEN: The early crow so early crows
That passes the night away
The trumpet shall sound and the dead shall be raised
At God's great judgement day
The hedges and fields are dotted in green
As green as the early leaf
Our heavenly father waters them
With his morning dew so sweet.

[*CLARKSON takes a deep breath and half gropes, half gooses MRS MAIDLEY. She gasps and the song stops. CLARKSON is smiling and serene.*]

CLARKSON: Praise the Lord.

MRS MAIDLEY: I'll praise him all right.

[*MRS MAIDLEY hits CLARKSON with an item of wet washing.*]

CLARKSON: Wait a minute. Wet washing in November. There's soldiers died of that.

[*CLARKSON disentangles himself.*]

Fellow creature...

MRS MAIDLEY: Fellow creature? With you?

MRS STEWER: Call the men, Mrs Colton.

MRS COLTON: I don't think we need them.

MRS STEWER: No. No. Come to think we can pay him out ourselves, the disgusting swine.

MRS COLTON: We can. We can give him a nice bit of scripture.

CLARKSON: Scripture? Scripture is no more than a ballad. Moses concocted the whole story.

[*They gasp. CLARKSON holds out his hands.*]

My one flesh. Are you the digging Levellers? What's thy name?

MRS COLTON: Don't tell him.

MRS MAIDLEY: Mrs Maidley.

CLARKSON: Was it a sin to touch you?

MRS STEWER: I think he's one of them Ranters.

MRS COLTON: So do I.

CLARKSON: So do I. I'm Lawrence Clarkson. I was told that some of my brethren dwelt with you here in Cobham.

MRS COLTON: No. We threw them out.

CLARKSON: Why?

MRS COLTON: They wouldn't work.

MRS STEWER: They started fights among our men.

MRS COLTON: They just lay about and got drunk.

CLARKSON: What thought you of them, Mrs Maidley?

[*Silence.*]

MRS COLTON: He's a Ranter. I'm going back to the huts.

[*MRS COLTON goes.*]

MRS STEWER: We don't want you. Stay away.

[*MRS STEWER goes. CLARKSON looks at the others. They go. Only MRS MAIDLEY is left.*]

CLARKSON: Mrs Maidley?

[*Silence.*]

Have you not seen man after man in the street and on this common and yearned to touch him and to be touched by him and yet you have not? Why haven't you?

MRS MAIDLEY: It's a sin.

CLARKSON: Sin. Did God make the world?

MRS MAIDLEY: Yes.

CLARKSON: Did he make all the creatures in it?

MRS MAIDLEY: Yes.

CLARKSON: Then whatever sins I commit God was the author of them all, and acted them in me.

[*CLARKSON caresses her. She does not stop him.*]

I'd sell all religions for a jug of beer. Those are most perfect, Mrs Maidley, that commit the greatest sins with least remorse.

[*CLARKSON kisses her.*]

MRS MAIDLEY: Have you any ribbons in your pack?

CLARKSON: Aye.

MRS MAIDLEY: Give me one.

CLARKSON: Why?

MRS MAIDLEY: There's nothing pretty about digging, is there?

CLARKSON: I cannot give you one.

MRS MAIDLEY: I say you can.

CLARKSON: I say no. For I must be careful for moneys for my wife.

MRS MAIDLEY: Your wife?

CLARKSON: Aye.

[*MRS MAIDLEY's instinct is to strike him again. He smilingly and gently evades it.*]

CLARKSON: Fellow creature: did I enquire of you about Mr Maidley?

MRS MAIDLEY: You – no.

CLARKSON: No. Yet you must choose. For among us it is the women who choose whom they will lie with.

MRS MAIDLEY: The women?

CLARKSON: There is deep love, Mrs Maidley, and there are the stirrings of the flesh. Since God is in our flesh as much as He was in Christ's – if there is a God, and if there was a Christ – let the stirrings speak one to the other.

MRS MAIDLEY: Does your wife choose whom she will have?

CLARKSON: Aye. For we have both found the truth that is within us.

MRS MAIDLEY: Where is she?

CLARKSON: In London.

MRS MAIDLEY: Do you go there to join her?

CLARKSON: I have been preaching the word. I go now to our house of God.

MRS MAIDLEY: To a church?

CLARKSON: Nay, fellow creature: to a tavern.

MRS MAIDLEY: Have you been a soldier?

CLARKSON: I'm a Captain.

MRS MAIDLEY: Never.

CLARKSON: Yea. I am the Captain of the Rant. I have my headquarters behind those bushes.

[*They laugh, and run away together to make love.*]

SCENE FOURTEEN

COBHAM
November, 1649

The Digger Camp. It is early evening of the same day. A silence as everybody pretends to be busy with their own affairs – but actually they are waiting for MRS MAIDLEY to return. Then she does return. People nudge each other. Someone giggles. MRS MAIDLEY sees MAIDLEY watching her.

MRS MAIDLEY: Here. Chestnuts. I found some late chestnuts. [*MAIDLEY walks up to her and hits her.*] Oh!

MRS COLTON: Oh, I felt that myself!

COLTON: It was no more than his duty.

STEWER: Cuckolds do hit hardest, don't they?

MAIDLEY: Shut up.

[*MAIDLEY hits MRS MAIDLEY again. She falls down. He kicks her.*]

MRS MAIDLEY: Oh... Oh...!

WINSTANLEY: Maidley. No more.

MAIDLEY: Will you fight me?

WINSTANLEY: Truly, tyranny in one is tyranny as well as in another. In a poor man lifted up by his valour as in a rich man lifted up by his lands.

[*MAIDLEY kicks MRS MAIDLEY again.*]

MRS MAIDLEY: Oh...!

WINSTANLEY: No more.

MAIDLEY: Think of me, did you? Think of people laughing at me, did you? Think of my feelings, did you? Think at all did you? Did you think at all?

[*MAIDLEY kicks MRS MAIDLEY.*]

MRS MAIDLEY: Oh...!

WINSTANLEY: No more!

MAIDLEY: Did she do wrong?

[*Silence.*]

Did she do wrong?

WINSTANLEY: I said no more.

MAIDLEY: Oh, you want Ranters do you? Are they the promised opportunity?

[*Silence. MRS STEWER moves to help MRS MAIDLEY.*]

You leave her.

MRS STEWER: Eh?

MAIDLEY: I said leave her.

[*They all watch in silence as MRS MAIDLEY recovers her breath and with pain and humiliation climbs to her feet. Eventually MAIDLEY speaks.*]

Get my dinner.

MRS MAIDLEY: No. [*MAIDLEY hits her.*] Oh!

MAIDLEY: Bitch. Whore.

MRS STEWER: Stop it.

MAIDLEY: Shut up.

WINSTANLEY: Maidley!

[*This time MAIDLEY sees that in the opinion of the group he has done more than enough.*]

MAIDLEY: Aye. I ask your pardon, brethren. I hope you'll pardon me for having been wronged. Now let her get my dinner.

[*There is an attempted return to the business of the evening. But MRS MAIDLEY checks it.*]

MRS MAIDLEY: No she will not get his dinner.

MAIDLEY: Eh?

MRS MAIDLEY: No she won't. She won't. She won't. She won't live in this pig-dirt muck-heap any more.

[*MAIDLEY turns on her. She throws the chestnuts at him. He instinctively dodges.*]

MAIDLEY: Look out!

MRS MAIDLEY: Turn the world upside down, will you?

MAIDLEY: Eh?

MRS MAIDLEY: Await the opportunity? See Christ in other creatures? See him in me!

MAIDLEY: Don't be stupid!

MRS MAIDLEY: Do I decide when I bleed? Eh? Do I? Eh? Do I?

MAIDLEY: What are you talking about?

MRS MAIDLEY: Do I decide that I'll bleed every month?

[*Silence.*]

Do I decide when you'll have me? Eh?

MAIDLEY: Shut up.

MRS MAIDLEY: Do I though? Eh? Do I decide when I'll get pregnant? Decide when I burst open with it coming out of me? Decide on my milk do I? Decide on him sucking me? Did I? Eh? Did I decide when he'd die?

[*Silence.*]

But I want to. I want me to decide.

MAIDLEY: You're mad. She's gone mad. You're mad.

MRS MAIDLEY: Aye. I want the world turned upside down.

WINSTANLEY: That's not mad.

MRS MAIDLEY: Then let me choose. Not men. Let me choose.

MRS COLTON: You can't choose Ranters.

MRS MAIDLEY: Why not?

MRS COLTON: You know why not.

MRS STEWER: They won't work.

MRS MAIDLEY: You told them I'd gone with Clarkson.

MRS STEWER: Ranters are disgusting.

WINSTANLEY: No. They are fellow creatures, but they will obey no rules, so they inflame men's hearts to quarrelling.

MRS MAIDLEY: What are your rules, Winstanley?

WINSTANLEY: We are peaceable, and decide by common consent.

MRS MAIDLEY: What are your rules? What's your punishment for having struck a woman?

[*Silence.*]

Turn the world upside down. Let me choose who I'll have, and throw them away in the morning.

[*Silence.*]

MRS COLTON: Men kill you if you say things like that. They kill you.

STEWER: You daft bitch. Why not do what you want anyway? Have you never heard of kiss and don't tell?

MRS MAIDLEY: Aye: for if you tell men kill you.

[*Silence.*]

WINSTANLEY: Truly: your Saviour must be a power within you to deliver you from such bondage within.

MRS MAIDLEY: Aye. Has he delivered you?

[*Silence. MRS MAIDLEY turns to go.*]

MAIDLEY: Where d'you think you're going?

MRS MAIDLEY: If you try to hold me I'll kill you in your sleep.

[*Silence.*]

WINSTANLEY: Fellow creature: where are you going?

MRS MAIDLEY: To enlist.

STEWER: Eh?

MRS MAIDLEY: With the Captain of the Rant.

SCENE FIFTEEN

CHESTER

December, 1649

A tavern yard. The low-life Cavaliers FURIOSITY, THEOBALD, LUCINDA and SNAPJOINT dance on to the tune of Over The Hills And Far Away.

FURIOSITY: I am Montmorency de Vere Quincy Salterton Jones-Jones Hampshire. Known by the nom de guerre Captain Furiosity.

[*Sings.*]

Were I one of Cromwell's saints
I would live in eternal joy
But my heart for money faints
So damn their eyes with false employ.

LUCINDA: I'm Lucinda, a very young and very merry whore.

[*Sings.*]

Were I born a rich lady
To no one husband I'd be true
For a better remedy
Is to buy up young men two by two.

THEOBALD: I am Theobald, the mad Cavalier.

[*Sings.*]

So take the road and away we go
Cheat and rob and kiss and play.

[*SNAPJOINT the battered wrestler is more slow witted.*]

SNAPJOINT: Am I Snapjoint, yes or no?

ALL: Yes!

[*Sing.*]

So over the hills and far away
Over the hills and far away!

THEOBALD: Quickly! He's coming! Take your places!

[*SNAPJOINT hides. THEOBALD and LUCINDA assume the postures of the blind doctor and his dutiful wife. FURIOSITY usher in CAPTAIN JONES of the New Model Army.*]

FURIOSITY: There, my dear friend Captain Jones, is the woman of whom I spoke. She is of noble birth, and was formerly the grand amour of His Majesty's leader of cavalry Lord Goring.

JONES: Lord Goring?

FURIOSITY: Yes.

JONES: Never.

FURIOSITY: I assure you. Yet her true fancy is not for high born men or sonneteers. Alas, fair nymph Lucinda! That she despises. She wants sweaty persons of the mob, such as yourself.

JONES: Me?

FURIOSITY: Grapple with her, sir. Grapple.

JONES: I can't.

FURIOSITY: Why not?

JONES: I don't know how. Not with a real lady.

FURIOSITY: You are an officer.

JONES: I used to be a buttonmaker.

FURIOSITY: Then you'll know how to unbutton, won't you?

JONES: Who's that man?

FURIOSITY: Man? What man? Oh, that man. That's her husband.

JONES: Eh?

FURIOSITY: Doctor Compass, the blind cartographer.

JONES: Blind?

FURIOSITY: How now, Doctor Compass?

THEOBALD: Furiosity?

FURIOSITY: Over here.

JONES: Blind?

FURIOSITY: Approach her.

[*JONES embraces LUCINDA. She warmly responds.*]

JONES: He really is blind!

LUCINDA: Mm...!

THEOBALD: Is someone there?

FURIOSITY: Here? Memories, Doctor. Memories and other fallen leaves.

THEOBALD: I sailed to the edge of the world, sir, and fell off. I was asleep. When I awoke my ship had become a bird's nest.

JONES: Oh... Ah...!

LUCINDA: Mm...!

[*FURIOSITY waves for SNAPJOINT, who walks up to JONES and taps him on the shoulder. JONES looks round from his embrace.*]

JONES: Clear off.

SNAPJOINT: No.

JONES: Eh?

LUCINDA: He's my husband's servant.

JONES: He's what?

SNAPJOINT: If you don't want me to tell, give me your money.

JONES: Take it off me.

LUCINDA: Eh?

JONES: I said: let him take it off me.

SNAPJOINT: Right.

FURIOSITY: Now for the sausage-meat.

[*SNAPJOINT lifts JONES in a fearsome wrestling hold. But halfway through SNAPJOINT locks his back and howls in pain.*]

SNAPJOINT: Oh! Ah! Ow!

THEOBALD: Good God, will you look at the stupid beast?

JONES: Look at him?

FURIOSITY: A metaphor, blowing in the wind!

JONES: He's not blind at all.

SNAPJOINT: Oh! Ah! My back's gone.

JONES: Who are you?

THEOBALD: I am Manfredi, the Neapolitan astrologer.

JONES: Manfredi? There's a warrant for him in Wrexham.

THEOBALD: *Je ne suis pas Manfredi. Je suis le chef du Roi de France.*

JONES: The French juggler?

FURIOSITY: Chef, sir. Chef. *Avec les* kitchens.

JONES: Kitchen? There's a warrant for him in Dolgelly.

LUCINDA: You great big hypocritical fool.

JONES: Me? There's warrants out for all of you.

LUCINDA: Come inside and I'll give you a quick one.

JONES: How much?

FURIOSITY: Gratis.

JONES: Eh?

LUCINDA: Nothing.

JONES: Then you'll leave the parish limits?

THEOBALD: We will – and you'll say nothing.

JONES: Done.

[*JONES and LUCINDA go inside.*]

FURIOSITY: Snapjoint. You're a broken man.

SNAPJOINT: Oh! Ah! Ow!

THEOBALD: Throw him away.

FURIOSITY: Throw away a friend? I'm a gentleman of fortune, sir, and I promised that I would see him settled, as any decrepit servant should be.

SNAPJOINT: I'll be right, sir. I'll be my old self with a massage.

FURIOSITY: What he needs is Jesus.

SNAPJOINT: Jesus?

FURIOSITY: I must let you go, Snapjoint. Jesus needs you.

THEOBALD: The Lord will provide.

SNAPJOINT: Has He told you? Say yes or no.

THEOBALD: Amen.

FURIOSITY: Jesus needs you, old friend. Jesus needs you.

SNAPJOINT: By heck.

[*SNAPJOINT holds out clenched fists. He begins to shake and whistle. He goes, exalted.*]

THEOBALD: I'd not have believed it.

FURIOSITY: My dear Theobald, as the King said at his execution, it's simply a matter of caring about the common scum and knowing what to give them.

THEOBALD: Sir, I have failed as an actor, a poet, a soldier and a criminal. Where is my next shilling to come from?

FURIOSITY: It is my opinion, sir, that if we can find ship to them, men of our stamp might make a very liberal fortune in the Colonies.

SCENE SIXTEEN

THE RANT
December, 1649

The David and Harp is a ranter tavern in Moor Lane, St Giles Cripplegate, in the City of London.

[*The LANDLORD MIDDLETON is with his wife MARY and MRS CLARKSON. Others present are SNAPJOINT,*

BAUTHUMLEY, COPPIN and JACKSON. CLARKSON enters with MRS MAIDLEY. He goes to his wife.]

CLARKSON: Fellow creatures.

MRS CLARKSON: Lawrence.

CLARKSON: My dear wife.

[*CLARKSON kisses his wife.*]

MARY: Lawrence.

[*CLARKSON kisses MARY.*]

CLARKSON: This is Mrs Maidley. My wife. Mary, and her husband Middleton.

MRS CLARKSON: Have you travelled with him?

MRS MAIDLEY: Aye.

MRS CLARKSON: Has he brought my money?

MRS MAIDLEY: Aye. He'd not spend it on me.

[*MIDDLETON gives MRS MAIDLEY a mug.*]

MIDDLETON: Here. This is the blood of Christ.

MRS MAIDLEY: Beer?

CLARKSON: Drink it.

[*MRS MAIDLEY hesitates. Then she raises the mug to them.*]

MRS MAIDLEY: Fellow creatures – isn't that what I should call you?

MRS CLARKSON: Aye.

[*They drink.*]

COPPIN: Sack, sister. Sack is the true divinity.

JACKSON: Nay. Tobacco.

COPPIN: Aye. Tobacco is a good creature.

SNAPJOINT: Yet, of all things, we see Christ better by
    drunkenness.

COPPIN: We do.

BAUTHUMLEY: Brother Middleton, have you meat,
    Brother Middleton? Have you the body of Christ?

MIDDLETON: Aye. It's on the spit.

SNAPJOINT: Is not God in man and beast, fish and fowl
    and every green thing from the highest cedar to the
    ivy on the wall?

JACKSON: He must be, for if not, where doth he sit with
    his arse?

MRS MAIDLEY: They like me. They're not bitches at
    all.

CLARKSON: What did I tell thee?

MRS MAIDLEY: I can't believe it.

CLARKSON: You have found the truth.

    [*COPPE enters with LUCY the maid.*]

COPPE: The day of the Lord!

CLARKSON: Hallelujah, Brother Coppe!

MIDDLETON: There is the body of Christ. Eat.

COPPIN: Eat the tree of life.

BAUTHUMLEY: Be at supper.

SNAPJOINT: Drink his blood and make you merry.

CLARKSON: Love: my one flesh: dwell with God. For
    in the grave there is no remembrance of either joy or
    sorrow after.

SHOUTS: Yea Lord. Amen. Yea Lord.

SNAPJOINT: God is in the sideboard.

JACKSON: Yea Lord.

[*Whistle. Quivers. Stamping. The atmosphere is building.*]

SNAPJOINT: If I should worship the sun or the moon or that pewter pot on the table nobody has anything to do with it.

MARY: Yea Lord.

COPPE: We will not live by the sword. We scorn to fight for anything. We had as lief be dead drunk every day of the week and lie with whores in the market place.

CLARKSON: My one flesh.

COPPE: We account them as good actions as taking the poor abused enslaved ploughman's money from him.

JACKSON: A pox on your prayers.

COPPE: We will not kill men.

MIDDLETON: Be with Christ.

COPPE: I will tell thee one hint more. There's swearing ignorantly in the dark, and there's swearing in the light, gloriously.

CLARKSON: Yea Lord and buggeration!

COPPE: I would rather hear a mighty angel swear a full-mouthed oath than an orthodox minister preach.

COPPIN: Give us your oaths.

BAUTHUMLEY: Speak it with God.

SNAPJOINT: Be as holy as God.

SHOUTS: Bums! Yea Lord! Tits! Nipples! Yea nipples! Arseholes! No sin!

[*The shouts become a song as the ranters link arms over their shoulders and, stamping to build a hypnotic rhythm, move in an ever-quickening circle.*]

Fellow creatures let me hear you
Yea Lord Yea Lord
Witness all and nothing fear
Yea Lord Yea
The Lord is in my skin and bone
Yea Lord Yea Lord
The Lord has made me all his own
Yea Lord Yea
The Lord is in the ale and meat
Yea Lord Yea Lord
He's in my hands He's in my feet
Yea Lord Yea
He's in my blood He's in my tears
Yea Lord Yea Lord
He's in my eyes He's in my ears
Yea Lord Yea
The Lord is in between my thighs
Yea Lord Yea Lord
He stiffens me and makes me rise
Yea Lord Yea
Come O Lord O let Him come
Yea Lord Yea Lord
In my loins Thy will be done
Yea Lord Yea

[*The circle whirls apart. The ranters are whooping and shouting. They tear their clothes off. COPPE and COPPIN whirl a skipping rope. The naked LUCY leaps up and down over it. The other women have chosen their men and they ardently make love.*]

SHOUTS: No sin! No sin! No sin!

COPPE: In the Kingdom of Christ which is a free Kingdom there is no sin unpardoned!

[*CLARKSON exults in the middle of it.*]

CLARKSON: Yea Lord! My humanity sups with humanity! I am the Captain of the Rant!

[*Tremendous drumming signifies the arrival of the forces of the law. People scream and scatter. Only CLARKSON and poor SNAPJOINT are left, to carry over into the next scene.*]

SCENE SEVENTEEN

BLASPHEMY
August, 1650

A courthouse.

[*The Magistrate is CAPTAIN KIRBY, now in civilian clothes. CLARKSON and SNAPJOINT face him.*]

KIRBY: Clarkson? Are you Lawrence Clarkson?

CLARKSON: Yes sir.

KIRBY: You are charged under the Blasphemy Acts of January and August of this year of our Lord 1650.

CLARKSON: Yes sir. I recanted, sir. I signed the paper, sir.

KIRBY: Is this it?

CLARKSON: Yes sir.

KIRBY: Have you anything else to say?

CLARKSON: Well, my money ran out, sir.

KIRBY: Your money?

CLARKSON: My army money.

KIRBY: I don't understand.

CLARKSON: I'll have to find work, sir.

KIRBY: Instead of preaching?

CLARKSON: Yes, sir.

KIRBY: You've been very silly, Clarkson.

CLARKSON: I know, sir.

KIRBY: Telling lies and stealing other men's wives. Very silly.

CLARKSON: I know, sir.

KIRBY: You'll stay in prison for a month – and then go home to your wife and behave yourself.

CLARKSON: Yes sir. Thank you, sir. I'm a quieter man now, sir.

KIRBY: Put him down.

[*CLARKSON is taken away – and leaves behind him perhaps, a shadow of a fist-clench, and the fading echo of a whistle.*]

[*Drums. SNAPJOINT is put up.*]

Who are you?

SNAPJOINT: Snapjoint, sir.

KIRBY: You are charged under the Blasphemy Acts of January and August of this year of our Lord 1650.

SNAPJOINT: Am I guilty? Say yes or no.

KIRBY: Do you realise that I'm a Justice of the Peace?

SNAPJOINT: Eh?

KIRBY: Did you say that you were Jesus Christ?

SNAPJOINT: I am.

KIRBY: You are Jesus Christ?

SNAPJOINT: Yes.

[*Silence.*]

I was matched once against a polar bear. And I threw
him.

KIRBY: I'll give you one more chance.

SNAPJOINT: Captain Furiosity said look for Christ, and
what he meant was pretend, and make people give
me money. But I thought about it. Christ is in every
man. I am Christ.

KIRBY: I want to be lenient if I can, Snapjoint.

SNAPJOINT: Jesus Christ. Say yes or no.

KIRBY: Guilty. You'll stand in the pillory and have a nail
driven through your tongue.

[*SOLDIERS put SNAPJOINT's arms over a cross-piece
and an iron muzzle over his face. Then they march him off.
We hear the song that carries over into the next scene.*]

What wondrous love is this
O my soul, O my soul
What wondrous love is this
O my soul
What wondrous love is this
That caused the Lord of bliss
To bear the dreadful curse
For my soul, for my soul
To bear the dreadful curse
For my soul
As I was sinking down
Sinking down sinking down
As I was sinking down
Sinking down

As I was sinking down
Beneath God's righteous ground
Christ laid aside his crown
For my soul, for my soul
Christ laid aside his crown
For my soul
And when from death I'm free
I'll sing on, I'll sing on
And when from death I'm free
I'll sing on
And when from death I'm free
I'll sing and joyful be
Through all eternity
For my soul, for my soul
Through all eternity
For my soul.

SCENE EIGHTEEN

PIRTON
September, 1650

WINSTANLEY and a group of diggers have been getting in the harvest for the rich and eccentric landowner LADY ELEANOR DAVIES. It is evening in her orchard at Pirton. The diggers file slowly past her to deposit the produce and collect their wages. The song ends when the last digger has been paid.

LADY ELEANOR: Winstanley. I can't keep you on. I can't afford it.

WINSTANLEY: I know.

LADY ELEANOR: I'm sorry. I've done my utmost.

[*Silence.*]

Where will you go?

WINSTANLEY: Where the majority decides.

[*Silence.*]

LADY ELEANOR: The bailiff says you have a grand design for a pamphlet.

WINSTANLEY: Yes.

LADY ELEANOR: Your plan for the commonwealth, he says.

WINSTANLEY: Yes.

LADY ELEANOR: What sort of a nation do you see?

WINSTANLEY: Oh, I see a nation that lives within itself: its merchants do not travel by sea and land to make slaves of other nations: I see a nation of plantations each governing itself: we will elect magistrates to administer and postmasters to exchange information with other plantations. We will educate both men and women. But we will not have lawyers. Take a cobbler from his seat or a butcher from his shop or any other tradesman that is an honest and just man and let him hear the case.

LADY ELEANOR: What sort of cases do you think they will be?

WINSTANLEY: Offences may arise from the spirit of unreasonable ignorance: from such as Ranters, who in seeking their own freedom embondage others.

LADY ELEANOR: Would you have an army?

WINSTANLEY: Once I would have said not.

[*Silence.*]

COLTON: Winstanley: there's somebody coming.

[*It is MRS MAIDLEY, looking very ill.*]

WINSTANLEY: Mrs Maidley? Fellow creature.

[*WINSTANLEY goes to greet her but checks when he sees that she is disfigured.*]

What ails you?

COLTON: What d'you think ails her? She's got the pox, hasn't she?

MRS MAIDLEY: Do I disgust you?

[*Silence.*]

WINSTANLEY: He's not here. Maidley's not here.

[*Silence.*]

We were scattered. A mob of people from Cobham attacked us. They burned our houses while the soldiers looked on. Then the soldiers chased us to the parish boundary. So there's just this few of us working for wages.

[*Silence.*]

LADY ELEANOR: Were you the Ranter?

MRS MAIDLEY: Yes.

LADY ELEANOR: Do you regret it?

MRS MAIDLEY: No.

LADY ELEANOR: Good for you.

WINSTANLEY: Cromwell picked off your leaders like flies. They all recanted.

[*MRS MAIDLEY shrugs.*]

COLTON: Leave her alone.

WINSTANLEY: Nay, I won't harm her, for I have never ceased to think about her. Were we alive – were any of us open and alive - on the day that Mrs Maidley ran off with the Captain of the Rant?

MRS COLTON: Let me tell you Winstanley that – No. No. I was jealous of her so I told her husband.

WINSTANLEY: I was shocked. I think I was frightened. I used fine words and sentiments as an excuse for not acting.

COLTON: Well – well I just thought: what if this happened to me, eh? What if I was made a public laughing-stock?

MRS COLTON: I knew it. That's all you think about. I knew it.

WINSTANLEY: And the moment has passed, as we have learned those moments do, in a rush of action. Action is the life of all. God is an active power, not an imaginary fancy.

COLTON: Of course he is.

MRS MAIDLEY: Give me the time over again, and I'd not go with Maidley in the first place.

[*Silence.*]

WINSTANLEY: Even with you, Lady Eleanor, there is an inward bondage because you pay us wages.

LADY ELEANOR: I know. I can't help it. I've done my utmost.

WINSTANLEY: At least we have the money from those wages. We can buy tools and dig again with more open hearts.

COLTON: No.

WINSTANLEY: Colton?

COLTON: Look. I've told you every day. I want to take my money and clear off.

WINSTANLEY: You said you'd consider it.

MRS COLTON: We have done.

WINSTANLEY: I shall send my plan for the commonwealth to Cromwell. If he chooses to implement it that will be the opportunity.

COLTON: Cromwell's a tyrant.

WINSTANLEY: Some hearts must be kept open.

COLTON: Ours are open.

MRS COLTON: It's just that there's proper work to be had.

WINSTANLEY: Proper work?

MRS COLTON: What was there in digging? Raw fingers and soaking wet clothes.

WINSTANLEY: Proper work?

COLTON: They're building warships again. I can go back to the dockyard for very good money.

[*Silence.*]

Oh come on. We've talked about it.

WINSTANLEY: Aye. We have. I've no right to judge you.

[*He looks at the others.*]

What about you?

[*Silence.*]

Mrs Maidley?

MRS MAIDLEY: I thought you'd be well set here. But you're not, are you?

[*Silence. Then the diggers go. After a moment or two MRS MAIDLEY follows them. WINSTANLEY and LADY ELEANOR are alone.*]

WINSTANLEY: Colton's a good man. I shall travel with him to London.

LADY ELEANOR: In your commonwealth, will men always be alive?

WINSTANLEY: Yes.

LADY ELEANOR: Will you still send your plan to Cromwell?

WINSTANLEY: Yes.

LADY ELEANOR: What if he ignores it?

[*Silence.*]

What if nations, like people, do their utmost and without knowing it cease to be alive?

[*Silence.*]

Winstanley: what if Burford was an utmost? What if after Ireland and Scotland our masters conquer the world? What if they make this nation the richest there has ever been? What if for all Cromwell's glory the King must come into his own again?

[*Silence. LADY ELEANOR seems about to speak but does not. She feels chilly. The sun has almost gone. LADY ELEANOR goes. WINSTANLEY is alone.*]

WINSTANLEY: So I await the Lord's leisure with a calm silence.

[*A long silence. Then a babel of songs:* To Be a Pilgrim, Bright Morning Star, Babylon is Fallen, Stand Up Now. *Then a drum roll and a man and a woman's voice sing.*]

Remember man that thou art born to die
And to the judgement seat thy soul must fly
So let your sins be 'ere so great or small
They must appear before the God of all.

[*WINSTANLEY puts his hat on, and then resolutely goes.*]

So proud and lofty do some people go
Dressing themselves like players in a show
They patch and they paint and dress with idle stuff
As if God had not made them fine enough.

[*The stage is empty.*]

THE END

THE BOMB IN BREWERY STREET

CHARACTERS

CAPTAIN ROWLEY

LIEUTENANT FOSTER

CORPORAL WILLIAMS

NOBBY

BIFFO

THISTLE

SMITH

SLEEPING SOLDIER

YOUNG MICHAEL DONOVAN

BILLY TULLY

OLD MICHAEL DONOVAN

MRS KELLY

JULIAN MASSINGHAM

MRS BRADY

BRENDA BRADY

MR BRADY

SISTER WALLACE

FATHER TOM BOGAN

KURT

FRITZ

FRANK GRAHAM

The Bomb in Brewery Street was first performed at the Crucible Theatre, Sheffield, on May 8th, 1975, with the following cast:

SMITH, Noel Cameron
WILLIAMS, David Ellison
YOUNG MICHAEL DONOVAN, Niall Padden
CAPTAIN ROWLEY, Colin McCormack
FRANK GRAHAM, Stanley McGeagh
NOBBY, John Salthouse
BIFFO, Terry Gilligan
THISTLE, Kenneth Sicklen
MRS KELLY, Doreen Mantle
LIEUTENANT FOSTER, Robin Soans
BILLY TULLY, Patrick Duggan
OLD MICHAEL DONOVAN, Paul Farrell
SLEEPING SOLDIER, Niall Padden
JULIAN MASSINGHAM MP, Christopher Northey
MRS BRADY, Aideen O'Kelly
BRENDA BRADY, Stephanie Fayerman
MR BRADY, Patrick Duggan
SUSAN DOHERTY, Candida Doyle or Ann Kimpton
FATHER TOM BOGAN, Harry Towb
SISTER WALLACE, Doreen Mantle
KURT, Noel Cameron
FRITZ, Stanley McGeagh
AMBULANCEMAN, Christopher Northey
DIRECTOR: David Leland
DESIGNER: Bernard Culshaw
LIGHTING: Peter Barham
SOUND: Derrick Zieba

SCENES

SCENE ONE: BREEZE BLOCKS - B Platoon's Ops Room in Brewery Street.

SCENE TWO: FISH AND CHIPS - HQ Platoon's Post in the Infants' School.

SCENE THREE: SNATCH SQUAD - A Council House on the Catholic Estate.

SCENE FOUR: BLOODY AWFUL COUNTRY - HQ Platoon's barrack room in the Infant's School.

SCENE FIVE: A TURN FOR THE ARMY - A Council House on the Protestant Estate.

SCENE SIX: MUG SHOTS - A Ward in the Catholic Hospital.

SCENE SEVEN: TODAY'S NUMBERS - B. Platoon's Ops Room in Brewery Street.

SCENE EIGHT: CUL DE SAC - Outside Lock-Up Garages on the Catholic Estate

All in Belfast in the late Autumn of 1971 when the British Army hoped to defeat the Provisional IRA by the following spring.

SCENE ONE

BREEZE BLOCKS

The Ops Room of 'B' Platoon post is in an empty semi-detached Victorian house. Pin-ups. Naked bulb. Camp bed. Trestle table. Radios.

[CORPORAL SMITH is on duty at the radio. He is 18 and reading a newspaper. CORPORAL WILLIAMS is in a canvas chair. Both are in shirt sleeves. An atmosphere of boredom and routine. One of the phones rings. SMITH answers it without excitement. He knows who it will be.]

SMITH: Ops Room... Hang on. It's Sammy at the OP. He says the Corporation workmen are here. Two fellers and a van.

WILLIAMS: What time is it?

SMITH: Midday.

WILLIAMS: They're early.

SMITH: Are they?

WILLIAMS: Better carry on, anyhow.

SMITH: [*To phone.*] ...Right... Carry on, Sammy... and you, you Wolverhampton cunt... [*He puts one phone down and lifts another, turning a handle to make it ring at the other end.*] ...Guard Room? Bertie One here. The Corporation workmen have arrived... Eh?... Right. Wilco... [*Puts down the phone.*] He says he'll tell Mr. Doherty next door.

WILLIAMS: Have you been in there?

SMITH: Next door?

WILLIAMS: Yes.

SMITH: No.

WILLIAMS: It's amazing. There's no furniture. Bags of holy pictures and Pope John, but no furniture.

SMITH: There's none in a lot of them, is there, from what the lads say.

WILLIAMS: You know what they are, don't you?

SMITH: Who?

WILLIAMS: The Irish.

SMITH: No, what?

WILLIAMS: Wogs in houses. Well, don't you think so?

SMITH: I don't know.

WILLIAMS: Why not?

SMITH: I've not been abroad before, have I?

WILLIAMS: What's that got to do with it?

SMITH: I've no comparisons.

WILLIAMS: I'm telling you. I've seen sights here that I wouldn't have thought possible in the UK. One place: nothing in the room, except all the clothes piled in the middle. Another: kids crapping in the corner. Another: two beds pulled together and three young lads sleeping crossways. I'm telling you. This is a bloody foreign country.

[*We hear the voice of MICHAEL, one of the Corporation workmen.*]

MICHAEL: [*Off.*] Is it up here? Is this where it is?

SMITH: I like them actually.

WILLIAMS: Who?

SMITH: The Irish.

WILLIAMS: I'm not saying I don't like 'em. I'm saying...

[*MICHAEL enters. He is about 18, in a donkey jacket and working jeans and battered gumboots.*]

MICHAEL: Excuse me. Can the officer sign this paper?

WILLIAMS: Who are you?

MICHAEL: Works Department.

WILLIAMS: The officer's not here.

MICHAEL: Oh...

WILLIAMS: How long will you be?... [*Before MICHAEL can answer he takes the paper and reads for himself.*] ...Breeze blocks. Metal rods. Bags of cement...

MICHAEL: That's another thing.

WILLIAMS: What?

MICHAEL: Your boys have stuck rods through the cement bags.

WILLIAMS: We must search them, lad – safety.

MICHAEL: It's carrying them in though.

SMITH: How d'you mean?

MICHAEL: They'll leak.

WILLIAMS: We can let you have some empty sandbags.

MICHAEL: Great. Thanks a million.

WILLIAMS: You're early aren't you? We were told tea-time.

MICHAEL: Er... my mate has to visit his wife in hospital, so we thought that if we finish early...

[*The 'phone rings again. SMITH answers.*]

SMITH: Ops. Room... Eh? Oh!

WILLIAMS: The family next door haven't been moved out yet so don't stack your material in the way, will you?

SMITH: It's Sammy again. He's admitted Mr Rowley and that bloke who owns the garage.

WILLIAMS: Oh, bloody no!

MICHAEL: Not trouble?

WILLIAMS: Just visitors.

SMITH: OK. Sammy...

MICHAEL: Look we've only the small van today so there are still half the breeze blocks and two sheets of corrugated iron to come. When we've stacked this load next door we'll be away to the depot for the corrugated and then maybe when we come back the officer could sign.

WILLIAMS: Sure. He's only out on foot patrol.

SMITH: D'you want a toffee?

MICHAEL: Oh... thanks a million.

SMITH: Take one for your mate.

MICHAEL: Thanks.

WILLIAMS: Carry on then.

MICHAEL: Thanks, you'll be well-protected when we've done.

[*MICHAEL goes.*]

WILLIAMS: Get Mr. Foster on patrol. Tell him Rowley's here.

SMITH: [*Using platoon radio.*] ...Bertie One to Bertie Three. Bertie One to Bertie Three. Do you read me?

[*Enter CAPTAIN ROWLEY, an officer of 27 or 28 and FRANK GRAHAM, a middle-class local civilian of perhaps 45.*]

ROWLEY: 'Morning Corporal. Who are these workmen?

WILLIAMS: They're blocking up the house next door, sir.

SMITH: [*To radio.*] I have Captain Rowley and a visitor here, sir.

ROWLEY: Is that Mr Foster?

SMITH: Yes, sir.

ROWLEY: Tell him it's about the publicity pictures.

SMITH: ...It's about the publicity pictures.

ROWLEY: This is Mr. Graham. You've heard a lot about him.

WILLIAMS: Hello, sir.

GRAHAM: Hello there. But surely there's people living next door?

ROWLEY: We're re-housing them. Then we seal off all doors and windows. It's the only way to make a post like this secure.

GRAHAM: Catholic family?

WILLIAMS: Yes, sir.

GRAHAM: Children?

WILLIAMS: Two little girls.

GRAHAM: Tragic. Tragic.

WILLIAMS: Cup of tea, sir?

GRAHAM: I will. Thank you... As Mrs Graham and I drove to the Golf Club Dance last night – it's a very pleasant function by the way...

ROWLEY: Yes...?

GRAHAM: Oh, yes. We take a big suite at the Conway
Hotel and they do us proud, I must say. You can let
your hair down – but tastefully, d'you know what I
mean? There's no slobs in there at all, in fact there's
some very cultured people – as Mrs. Graham and I
drove there we were stopped at an army road block
and they had us out of the car in our evening clothes.
Actually they were the soul of courtesy. The military
are. In view of the swinish provocation they've
received the military are most restrained and whoever
says otherwise is a liar. Of course Catholics are bloody
liars. Anyway they got us out of the car – put up with
these inconveniences I say, otherwise social life
collapses – and I turned to Mrs Graham, and I said:
it's all very well for us, we live in a decent district,
thank God (not that we haven't worked hard) but
when will it end? When will men of violence see
sense?

WILLIAMS: Er... d'you take sugar, sir?

GRAHAM: Four lumps. Thank you. You're doing a
grand job, all of you.

ROWLEY: Well if we can beat the IRA, and we will beat
them, peace talks can begin.

GRAHAM: Talks? Who with? What the hell is there to
say except that we're British and we want to stay
British?

ROWLEY: Er... anyway Mr Graham, about the photograph.

GRAHAM: Sure. Is this the room?

ROWLEY: No. This is the Ops. Room. We'll actually put
the TV in the platoon mess.

GRAHAM: How many reporters can you get?

ROWLEY: The national papers, BBC, Ulster TV.

GRAHAM: The main thing is for people over the water to see that there are still more decent people in Ulster than not.

[*'Phone rings. SMITH answers.*]

SMITH: Ops. Room... Thank you, Sammy... [*He hangs up.*] The workmen have gone. They'll be back in thirty minutes.

WILLIAMS: Have you logged them?

SMITH: Sure.

GRAHAM: What is this, I mean? A 23-inch colour television, the gift to your unit of businessmen and ordinary citizens of the district. A mark of our appreciation.

ROWLEY: We think it's tremendous community relations: good for the whole situation.

GRAHAM: It's a change from my army days.

ROWLEY: What?

GRAHAM: If you'd told me when I was a squaddie that I'd see myself with as big a garage as I own today I might have believed you, but if you'd said each regiment can appoint its own publicity officer – never!

ROWLEY: We think it admits a lot of daylight.

GRAHAM: God, the way the world's changed since I was a kid. If those IRA bastards knew that... if my own son knew it.

ROWLEY: To return to the photograph for a moment... The girl who actually hands over the TV set...

GRAHAM: Miss Belfast Motor Trades 1971.

ROWLEY: Yes.

GRAHAM: She works on my switchboard.

ROWLEY: She will be in her bikini, won't she?

GRAHAM: She will. She's got breasts like two footballs. Cultured girl as a matter of fact. She's got two or three 'O' Levels.

ROWLEY: We should make a lot of papers.

GRAHAM: It's social harmony. It's what it should all be about.

ROWLEY: I know that the unit are very eager for colour. Isn't that right, Corporal?

WILLIAMS: I'll say. It should make all the difference.

GRAHAM: Colour television? It's a new world. Mrs Graham and I we're old hands I can tell you, we've seen a thing or two – Mrs Graham, she was a nurse in a Catholic hospital, they come in from the peats not having washed for twenty years – but when she saw colour television for the first time she...

[*There is a blinding flash and then the lights go out as plastic bombs explode in the breeze blocks stacked next door. The back wall crashes into the room and the men are buried or blown over. Somewhere in the house a man starts screaming.*]

WILLIAMS: Smith. Will you stop screaming, Smith? What are you doing lad? Where are you?

ROWLEY: I want a numerical report, Corporal, and then every man in the water.

WILLIAMS: Hey. I can stand up. Smith. I can stand up.

[*Soldiers enter to help, led by NOBBY.*]

NOBBY: Come on get this shifted. It was those workmen. The bastards. The murdering filthy – oh. Is that
you Mr Rowley?

ROWLEY: I shall ask for your backstroke, Nobby: two
lengths of the bath.

WILLIAMS: Eh?

NOBBY: Concussed.

WILLIAMS: I never know with officers.

[*The screaming stops.*]

Smith? What's happened?

NOBBY: Where is he?

WILLIAMS: There.

NOBBY: Here? This isn't him.

WILLIAMS: Mr. Graham. Civilian...

NOBBY: A bloody dead one. Smith must be under that lot.

ROWLEY: Corporal: which way are the changing
rooms?

NOBBY: All right sir. I'm with you.

ROWLEY: I left my wrist watch with the attendant.

NOBBY: I know the drill sir. Big brown envelope.

WILLIAMS: Hey. What about me?

NOBBY: I'll come back for you.

WILLIAMS: I can bloody make my own way.

NOBBY: Argue, argue all the bloody time.

[*NOBBY helps ROWLEY off. Soldiers carry GRAHAM's
body. WILLIAMS hobbles himself. Fade.*]

SCENE TWO

FISH AND CHIPS

HQ platoon occupies half a modern infant's school on the Catholic housing estate and we are looking at a functional corridor, and one of the rooms which leads off it. The room was probably built as a staff room because it contains an armchair and bookshelves, but in this emergency it serves as CAPTAIN ROWLEY's bedroom. It contains his shaving things and family photos and a plastic travelling wardrobe on a metal frame. Now a second bed has been moved in, and some space roughly cleared, for LIEUTENANT FOSTER, the B platoon officer bombed out of Brewery Street. The corridor is functional: it has two canvas chairs with metal frames, a home-made educational chart of Our Friends the Birds *and two empty army jerricans.*

[*It is night. A local woman, MRS KELLY is brought along the corridor by THISTLE, a private soldier of HQ Platoon fully accoutred for duty.*]

THISTLE: Sit there.

[*The door of the Ops. Room is marked 'Ops. Room – Restricted'. THISTLE knocks and pops in his head.*]

Mrs Kelly, sir.

FOSTER: [*Off.*] Thank you.

[*THISTLE assumes a watching stance. Silence. Eventually MRS KELLY speaks...*]

MRS KELLY: Do you like it here?

THISTLE: Eh?

MRS KELLY: Living in the school.

THISTLE: I've seen worse.

MRS KELLY: I daresay.

THISTLE: ... [*Stolid. He doesn't want to be friends.*]

MRS KELLY: Have you children yourself.

THISTLE: Yes.

MRS KELLY: Then you'll know my feelings.

THISTLE: Yes.

[*Silence. Then THISTLE speaks again.*]

If you want a cigarette have one.

MRS KELLY: I didn't bring them.

THISTLE: Easily done.

[*Silence. Then MRS KELLY looks at THISTLE.*]

MRS KELLY: ... [*Unspoken question.*] ...?

THISTLE: I don't smoke.

[*Silence. Then FOSTER comes out of the Ops. Room. He is about as old as ROWLEY and has an open, honest face. He is wearing a khaki shirt and tie and camouflage trousers, and carries a clipboard.*]

FOSTER: Mrs Kelly?

MRS KELLY: Is there any news sir?

FOSTER: Sorry, I can't take you into the Ops. Room because it's restricted. There's no news yet, but I've put out a radio message and we're sending a special patrol.

MRS KELLY: What's that?

FOSTER: Just a few men.

MRS KELLY: Oh.

FOSTER: Would you like a cup of tea?

MRS KELLY: Oh, I sure would.

FOSTER: Sugar?

MRS KELLY: Thanks.

FOSTER: Thistle ...

> [*THISTLE's departure is checked by MRS KELLY's question.*]

MRS KELLY: Is the milk tinned?

FOSTER: Er...

MRS KELLY: I mean if you've only the tinned milk that's great by me.

> [*THISTLE goes.*]

Nice lad.

FOSTER: Yes.

MRS KELLY: I'd understand if a soldier wasn't – d'you know what I mean?

FOSTER: Mrs Kelly I know it can be very distressing to have to repeat a story but I haven't heard yours at first hand and there may be important details you've missed. What time was it when your daughter... Teresa?

MRS KELLY: Teresa.

FOSTER: What time did she go out?

MRS KELLY: Nine o'clock.

FOSTER: You're sure.

MRS KELLY: They were all watching the film on TV when the advertisements come on in the middle. Damien – he's my youngest son – Damien said what's for eats and I thought Jesus – d'you know that feeling – I thought Jesus I've nothing in so I gave Teresa a ten shillings but at first she wouldn't go.

Well that made me angry I can tell you. So in the end she did go...

[*Sudden distress and sobs.*] ...

FOSTER: Mrs Kelly I'm sure that whatever's happened it's not as bad as you fear.

MRS KELLY: ... [*Crying.*] ...

[*THISTLE arrives with a mug of tea.*]

THISTLE: Here you are. Tea.

MRS KELLY: ... [*Blows her nose.*] ...

THISTLE: Two sugars.

MRS KELLY: That's great. Really great.

FOSTER: So at nine o'clock you sent Teresa to the fish and chip shop.

MRS KELLY: I did.

FOSTER: And you live in Primrose Avenue.

MRS KELLY: Primrose Avenue.

FOSTER: How many chip shops still function up there?

MRS KELLY: Just the one sir.

THISTLE: Peter Fahy's.

MRS KELLY: Top of the Springfield Road.

FOSTER: That's very near your house.

MRS KELLY: It's three minutes – well with all the street lamps out, which they are, and all the muck and goings on in the street it's ten at the most.

FOSTER: So when after half an hour Teresa had failed to come home you were worried.

MRS KELLY: I was worried sick.

FOSTER: That was nearly two and a half hours ago.

MRS KELLY: ... [*No reply.*] ...

[*FOSTER and THISTLE exchange glances.*]

FOSTER: Did Teresa arrive at the chip shop?

MRS KELLY: No.

FOSTER: Are you sure?

MRS KELLY: First place I asked.

FOSTER: Who answered you?

MRS KELLY: Peter himself.

FOSTER: Can you trust him?

MRS KELLY: What d'you mean?

FOSTER: You know what I mean Mrs Kelly.

MRS KELLY: I want her back. That's all I want. I want my girlie.

[*Another exchange of glances between FOSTER and THISTLE. FOSTER decides upon another tack.*]

FOSTER: Teresa is fourteen years of age, about five feet tall, slim build, she was wearing a blue skirt, a white blouse and a blue school raincoat ...

MRS KELLY: Donkey jacket.

FOSTER: Oh, donkey jacket... You've checked friends' houses and ...

MRS KELLY: Yes.

FOSTER: Hm... There's nothing more you should tell us?

MRS KELLY: ... [*Shrug.*]

FOSTER: You're sure?

MRS KELLY: I've the other kids at home; will the TV have stopped now?

FOSTER: Yes. Are they on their own?

MRS KELLY: There's a good friend next door.

FOSTER: Where's your husband?

MRS KELLY: Peterborough.

THISTLE: Peterborough?

MRS KELLY: Sure.

FOSTER: He's working there?

MRS KELLY: He is.

FOSTER: Well... [*Indicating to THISTLE that he should keep watch on MRS KELLY.*] You'll have to wait here I'm afraid, until we do have some news.

[*CAPTAIN ROWLEY enters from outside, carrying some of his clothes over his arm.*]

ROWLEY: Evening Geoff.

FOSTER: Mike.

ROWLEY: Hello Thistle.

THISTLE: Evening, sir.

FOSTER: You're out of hospital.

ROWLEY: Yes.

FOSTER: How do you feel?

ROWLEY: Tremendous.

[*At the door of his room.*]

What's this?

FOSTER: Er... well, when the platoon was bombed out of Brewery Street they moved us in here with you.

ROWLEY: Are these your things?

FOSTER: Yes.

ROWLEY: Can't get away from you can I?

FOSTER: You don't mind do you?

ROWLEY: Good heavens no.

FOSTER: I've not really moved anything.

ROWLEY: Are you taking my Ops. Room duty?

FOSTER: Yes.

ROWLEY: Who is that woman?

FOSTER: Mrs Kelly. Primrose Avenue.

ROWLEY: Primrose Avenue?

FOSTER: Yes.

ROWLEY: My God.

FOSTER: Why?

ROWLEY: That's where Private Green was shot and while he lay on the pavement the women came out and blew rozzers at him and offered all the usual greetings.

FOSTER: Mother-fucking Tommy.

ROWLEY: Your wife's at home with a black man. So what does this harpy want?

FOSTER: Help.

ROWLEY: Never.

FOSTER: Her daughter went out for chips and hasn't come back.

ROWLEY: When?

FOSTER: Nearly three hours.

ROWLEY: Ambush?

FOSTER: Hardly.

ROWLEY: No, they'd just set a car on fire. Look at that. Explosion completely ripped my flak jacket.

FOSTER: It was plastic stuff in the breeze blocks. We've identified one of the supposed workmen.

ROWLEY: Which?

FOSTER: The boy.

ROWLEY: He's nothing.

FOSTER: Michael Donovan, from the Ardoyne.

ROWLEY: What about the other?

FOSTER: Sent up from Dublin.

ROWLEY: Who says so?

FOSTER: Usual formula, isn't it, when there's no photo?

ROWLEY: Do you want some of this wardrobe?

FOSTER: I think I'm all set, Mike, actually ...

ROWLEY: Are we getting after Donovan?

FOSTER: I think we're working on it.

ROWLEY: Hm... [*Jerking head to MRS KELLY.*] ...What d'you reckon then? Tar and feathers job?

FOSTER: Well ...

ROWLEY: How old is she?

FOSTER: Fourteen.

ROWLEY: Too young. They'd just beat her up. No help from mum I suppose.

FOSTER: None.

ROWLEY: Is she one of our informants?

FOSTER: The girl? Not that I know of.

ROWLEY: Wonder what she's done then ...

FOSTER: Stealing from shops?

ROWLEY: Could be.

FOSTER: I suppose that if it is an IRA law and order job she won't talk much to us.

ROWLEY: They don't as a rule. D'you want a nip from the flask?

FOSTER: Super...

[*ROWLEY pours FOSTER a nip.*]

Mike.

ROWLEY: Mm?

FOSTER: Have you heard from Sheila?

ROWLEY: Since the explosion? Yes, I talked to her on the phone.

FOSTER: Did she mention Marion?

ROWLEY: Of course.

FOSTER: How was she?

ROWLEY: Tremendous.

FOSTER: Good.

ROWLEY: Usual married quarters stuff. World shaking chats across the garden fence.

FOSTER: Should I wangle a permanent UK posting? What's your opinion?

ROWLEY: Geoffrey, I can't possibly decide.

FOSTER: We've been married four years and I've been with her for two. I've been with the baby for just five months.

ROWLEY: We all have to face it Geoffrey.

FOSTER: I don't think it makes a good basis for life. I really don't.

ROWLEY: ... [*A shrug. Polite, friendly, even affectionate. But setting a limit between one man's responsibilities and another's.*] ...

FOSTER: If I do apply will they know it's a wangle? I mean, how far will it stand against me later?

ROWLEY: I don't know.

FOSTER: You must have some idea Mike.

ROWLEY: I haven't. Each case is different.

FOSTER: But that is the problem isn't it — subsequent promotion?

ROWLEY: If you put it that way I suppose it is.

FOSTER: It's certainly what worries me. Marion doesn't care about these things. Or at least she says she doesn't. She seems to throw all that on me. I expect you've noticed.

ROWLEY: Shouldn't you get back to Ops. Room?

[*FOSTER returns to the Ops. Room passing as he does so MRS KELLY.*]

FOSTER: I'm checking for you now, Mrs Kelly.

[*FOSTER disappears into the Ops. Room. Silence. MRS KELLY looks at THISTLE but he ignores her. In his room ROWLEY sits down. He looks around. He accustoms himself*

*to being alone again among his possessions back from the
dead. A little wry and careful. Cheery whistling.
CORPORAL WILLIAMS enters from outside. He is in
civilian clothes. He knocks on the Ops. Room door and
pops his head in.*]

WILLIAMS: Reporting back, sir. Thank you.

[*WILLIAMS nods to THISTLE and is on his whistling
way when he sees that the light is on in ROWLEY's room.*]

[*An interrogatory gesture...*]

THISTLE: Yes. He's back.

WILLIAMS: [*Knocks on ROWLEY's door.*]

ROWLEY: Come.

WILLIAMS: How's the old invalid?

ROWLEY: Hello. Tremendous. Have a gasper. Why are
you in civvies?

WILLIAMS: I've been at the Community Dance.

ROWLEY: Any good?

WILLIAMS: The usual Protestant scrubbers.

ROWLEY: You mean they're as young as your daughter?

WILLIAMS: I didn't say so.

ROWLEY: Have they put you in with HQ Platoon?

WILLIAMS: The same bloody room. We're like battery
hens. And as for the toilets.

ROWLEY: What else do you expect?

WILLIAMS: They're made for small kids.

ROWLEY: It is an infant's school.

WILLIAMS: When I sit down my goolies touch the water.

ROWLEY: You're the best hung man in the Company.

WILLIAMS: If only I was...

ROWLEY: [*Between a laugh and a smile.*] ...

WILLIAMS: Anyway, I'm bloody glad to see you. I suppose you heard the final score?

ROWLEY: In the explosion?

WILLIAMS: Yes.

ROWLEY: Smith, Mr Graham, Mr Doherty next door and one of his two little girls.

WILLIAMS: The other one's in hospital.

ROWLEY: Bad?

WILLIAMS: Apparently...

[*FOSTER pops his head out of the Ops. Room.*]

FOSTER: Captain Rowley please.

THISTLE: Mr Rowley.

WILLIAMS: Hey up.

FOSTER: Nothing yet Mrs... er...

[*FOSTER pops back. ROWLEY goes from his own room to the Ops. Room. WILLIAMS comes out into the corridor.*]

WILLIAMS: Well, Thistle. I'm turning in.

THISTLE: How was the dance?

WILLIAMS: I'm too old for that kind of caper.

THISTLE: Have all the lads come back?

WILLIAMS: No. The RSM looked in on patrol so I pinched a lift.

THISTLE: This is Mrs Kelly from Primrose Avenue.

WILLIAMS: Primrose... That's where Wanker Green got his.

THISTLE: Yes.

WILLIAMS: I hit a woman with my riot stick.

THISTLE: ... [*Looks, says nothing.*] ...

WILLIAMS: Aye. Cut her head open.

MRS KELLY: ... [*Looks away.*] ...

THISTLE: Mrs Kelly's lost her daughter.

WILLIAMS: Dead?

THISTLE: Missing.

WILLIAMS: Oh. Well, she'll turn up.

MRS KELLY: Do you think so?

WILLIAMS: Positive. See you.

[*WILLIAMS nods to THISTLE and goes whistling to his bunk.*]

FOSTER: Well we've found your daughter Mrs Kelly.

MRS KELLY: Is she dead?

FOSTER: No of course not she's...

MRS KELLY: Is she marked?

FOSTER: Marked?

MRS KELLY: On her face?

FOSTER: No.

MRS KELLY: Then where is she?

FOSTER: We sent her home.

MRS KELLY: Sent her?

FOSTER: Escorted. A foot patrol found her in the Conville flats playground.

MRS KELLY: She's hurt and you won't tell me.

FOSTER: She's not hurt. She was with two youths.

MRS KELLY: What?

FOSTER: Two youths.

MRS KELLY: Who were they?

FOSTER: I don't know.

MRS KELLY: What were they doing?

FOSTER: Well... what do you think?

MRS KELLY: I don't believe it.

FOSTER: They ran away when they heard the soldiers.

MRS KELLY: Teresa and two... Let me tell you that at the gate of this post I was frisked by one of your men and that's not allowed, I know for a fact that a woman should be frisked by a woman.

FOSTER: Mrs Kelly if you...

MRS KELLY: A soldier put his hands on me in a most disgusting way.

FOSTER: I'll send you in a jeep Mrs Kelly.

MRS KELLY: I'll walk.

FOSTER: This way then.

MRS KELLY: Fucking British Army.

THISTLE: Come on.

[*THISTLE's hand is more to guide than to force but she shrugs it away.*]

MRS KELLY: Oh will you touch me will you?

[*MRS KELLY and THISTLE go. FOSTER turns to face the Ops. Room door at which ROWLEY appears.*]

ROWLEY: [*Mimicking.*] ... My Teresa and two youths...

FOSTER: [*Laughter.*]

ROWLEY: Randy little bitch. Why didn't she run off?

FOSTER: She was looking for her knickers.

ROWLEY: Oh Lord. Poor Mrs Kelly. Do you think the gate boys did frisk her?

FOSTER: Probably.

ROWLEY: Difficult decision.

FOSTER: I'd better check...

ROWLEY: Did you lose much gear in the explosion?

FOSTER: The cassette player Marion bought.

ROWLEY: I remember.

[*Silence.*]

Well I think I'll turn in Geoff.

[*FOSTER makes a last attempt to keep the contact.*]

FOSTER: Er...

ROWLEY: What?

FOSTER: Nothing. I... I was just thinking how we'd be if we lived in Primrose Avenue.

ROWLEY: Unemployed, or gone away to work...

FOSTER: Yes.

[*Silence.*]

ROWLEY: Well I suppose I'd better go for a pee.

[*ROWLEY walks off down the corridor. FOSTER is alone for a moment and then re-enters the Ops. Room.*]

SCENE THREE

SNATCH SQUAD

A council house on the Catholic estate in the dead black-becoming-grey early hours of the morning. A little light from a half curtained window. The only sound is that of someone snoring. Then there is a crash of breaking glass and then the light goes on.

[*Old BILLY TULLY wakes with a long gasping shout at what he sees. The room is full of armed and accoutred soldiers with blackened faces. CORPORAL WILLIAMS, NOBBY with the radio on his back, BIFFO and CAPTAIN ROWLEY.*]

ROWLEY: Get hold of him.

[*BIFFO grabs BILLY and clamps a hand over his mouth.*]

Shut the curtain.

[*NOBBY closes the curtain. We can grasp now that TULLY lives in the once pleasant but now barely furnished front room. There are two mattresses on the floor. TULLY was sleeping on one. The man on the other mattress has not even woken.*]

Is that him?

WILLIAMS: Must be.

ROWLEY: Keep him covered.

NOBBY: For Christ's sake be careful.

ROWLEY: All right Donovan the party's over.

WILLIAMS: Donovan.

ROWLEY: Get up.

WILLIAMS: Get up you bastard.

[*WILLIAMS rips off the covering. DONOVAN sits up. He is not the youth of the first scene but an old and bewildered man who, when he see the soldiers, starts to bellow.*]

ROWLEY: Stop him.

[*DONOVAN also is grabbed. Two old men with rough hands across their mouths.*]

WILLIAMS: He's not Michael Donovan.

ROWLEY: Are you sure?

WILLIAMS: Positive.

ROWLEY: Are you William Tully?

TULLY: ... [*Noise.*] ...

ROWLEY: Did you live in Bombay Street near the Shankhill?

TULLY: ... [*Noise.*] ...

ROWLEY: Your house was burned by Protestants so you moved up here. Is that correct?

TULLY: ... [*Noise.*] ...

ROWLEY: If the soldier lets you go will you answer quietly?

TULLY: ... [*Noise.*] ...

ROWLEY: Let him go.

[*BIFFO lets TULLY go.*]

TULLY: This is a fucking outrage and...

BIFFO: Shut up.

TULLY: I never left the front door open.

ROWLEY: I've a warrant under the Special Powers Act.

TULLY: I've done nothing.

ROWLEY: I'm snatching the pair of you.

TULLY: What's that noise?

ROWLEY: Noise?

WILLIAMS: It's Mr Foster sir. He's upstairs with the mine detector.

ROWLEY: Let the other man go...

[*DONOVAN is released and immediately starts to shout.*]

TULLY: Michael...

[*DONOVAN is grabbed and gagged again.*]

NOBBY: What the bloody hell is this?

ROWLEY: Now look here Tully...

TULLY: I don't care if you've fifty warrants...

ROWLEY: Don't argue.

TULLY: There's no call for a mine detector.

ROWLEY: Is this house yours?

TULLY: Certainly.

ROWLEY: Where's your rent book?

TULLY: Rent book?

ROWLEY: Rent book.

TULLY: Temporarily mislaid.

ROWLEY: What's wrong with this comedian?

TULLY: He's deaf.

WILLIAMS: Deaf?

DONOVAN: ... [*Noise.*] ...

NOBBY: Deaf.

ROWLEY: That's the first question. The second is can he understand you?

TULLY: Sure.

ROWLEY: Then explain what...

TULLY: Why should I?

ROWLEY: Because so far no-one knows we're here but if they find out and there's a riot you'll be hurt.

TULLY: Aye. There's some truth in that.

ROWLEY: If he keeps quiet he won't be harmed.

TULLY: Oh...

ROWLEY: Tell him.

TULLY: Right.

[*TULLY turns to DONOVAN and shouts at the top of his voice.*]

Can you hear me Michael?

WILLIAMS: Shut your...

NOBBY: He did that deliberate.

BIFFO: He'll ave 'em all round...

TULLY: I must engage his attention.

ROWLEY: Can he read?

TULLY: Of course he can read.

ROWLEY: Who is he anyway?

TULLY: Mr brother-in-law.

WILLIAMS: Michael Donovan?

TULLY: Eh?

WILLIAMS: Is his name Michael Donovan?

TULLY: Of course his name's Michael Donovan.

NOBBY: He's not just deaf though is he?

TULLY: He's had a fucking stroke hasn't he?

ROWLEY: Show him this.

  [*ROWLEY had written on his message pad.*]

TULLY: "Keep quiet and you will not be harmed..."
  Should you not sign it?

WILLIAMS: I'll sign your arse.

TULLY: Here Michael. Here you are son. Can you see
  it? Can you read it OK?

DONOVAN: ... [*Noise.*] ...

TULLY: Keep quiet and you will not be harmed.

DONOVAN: ... [*Noise.*]

TULLY: That's it son. We're not dead yet are we not by a
  long chalk.

DONOVAN: ... [*Noise.*] ...

TULLY: What? Oh. Will you pass his blanket?

BIFFO: Can I let him go?

TULLY: Sure you can.

  [*BIFFO lets DONOVAN go.*]

DONOVAN: ... [*Noise.*] ...

[*TULLY wraps the blanket round DONOVAN.*]

TULLY: There you are son. No, no. We're not dead yet
by a long chalk. [*To soldiers.*] British ex-servicemen.
Can you not tell?

NOBBY: No.

TULLY: His shoulders, Tommy. Irish Guards.

WILLIAMS: When was that?

TULLY: Nineteen Fifteen.

ROWLEY: Will you get yourselves dressed now Mr Tully
and collect your overnight belongings?

TULLY: I will not.

ROWLEY: Then we'll go as we are.

TULLY: Michael's no trousers on.

ROWLEY: Biffo, so long as Mr Foster's ready...

TULLY: Can we not talk this over Tommy?

ROWLEY: There's nothing to say.

TULLY: I'm not going in the dark.

WILLIAMS: Nobody saw us come in.

ROWLEY: We'll go through the allotments at the back.

TULLY: Get me out there and you'll beat me up.

WILLIAMS: You daft old bugger.

ROWLEY: We'll take them as they are Corporal.

TULLY: No. No I'll...

ROWLEY: Then get Donovan's trousers on first.

TULLY: If one of you holds him.

ROWLEY: Is he paralysed?

TULLY: Just a wee bit in the one leg.

ROWLEY: Does he attend a remedial clinic?

TULLY: A what?

ROWLEY: Where's his medical card?

TULLY: Ask him.

ROWLEY: Where's his pension book? Where's yours?

WILLIAMS: Don't need them, do they?

NOBBY: No.

WILLIAMS: Rob a bank or two.

NOBBY: Where does the money go?

WILLIAMS: Welfare Committee.

TULLY: What are you talking about?

WILLIAMS: You're a fucking no-go area.

BIFFO: Listen ...

[*All stop. Listen. All hear the dustbin lids beginning to rattle.*]

NOBBY: Oh bloody hell...

WILLIAMS: It's the dustbin lids.

TULLY: They know you're in here...

ROWLEY: Yes. Biffo see if Mr Foster's ready.

BIFFO: Yes sir.

[*BIFFO goes upstairs.*]

ROWLEY: Nobby get the vehicles up here.

NOBBY: Yes sir.

TULLY: If there's a riot I'm not moving.

NOBBY: Bertie Three to Bertie Four. Bertie Four do you read me?

WILLIAMS: Don't worry. You won't have to move.

TULLY: Eh?

WILLIAMS: They'll bring the riot here.

RADIO VOICE: Go ahead Bertie Four.

NOBBY: Bertie Three to Bertie Four. Sunrise-Sunrise. Bring saucepans to refrigerator.

TULLY: What's he talking about?

WILLIAMS: It's code isn't it?

RADIO VOICE: Bertie Three Wilco. Over.

NOBBY: Vehicles coming round sir.

ROWLEY: Thank you. Now Mr Tully, if...

NOBBY: Hang about.

WILLIAMS: What?

NOBBY: You've got 'em back to front.

WILLIAMS: No we haven't

NOBBY: Show me his flies.

WILLIAMS: Right.

   [*DONOVAN's trousers are hoisted up, wrong way round.*]

   Oh Jesus.

   [*Crash of glass as a brick breaks a window. The gathering crowd shouts.*]

NOBBY: Lights out sir?

ROWLEY: I think so.

WILLIAMS: Oh no...

NOBBY: What's up now.

WILLIAMS: They've set fire to something.

[*Glare outside. As the lights go off it illuminates the room. ROWLEY draws the curtain so that he can see.*]

What is it sir?

ROWLEY: Looks like an old sofa.

NOBBY: They've been saving it.

ROWLEY: Half of them are children. Fully dressed. I don't know where they find the energy.

[*BIFFO reappears.*]

BIFFO: Message from Mr Foster sir.

ROWLEY: Has he found something?

BIFFO: In the bathroom sir.

ROWLEY: What?

BIFFO: An M1 Carbine and fifty rounds and he's taking up more floorboards.

WILLIAMS: Hear that?

NOBBY: Carbine in the bathroom...

WILLIAMS: Ever been in there?

TULLY: You shut your gob.

NOBBY: You're a scruffy old sod.

TULLY: I said shut your gob.

NOBBY: Listen we've got fucking napalm at home you know.

WILLIAMS: Never mind sofas and school kids.

NOBBY: You want to learn about real war.

WILLIAMS: We could blast this wog city in two minutes.

NOBBY: Well actually that was an exaggeration.

WILLIAMS: Eight minutes.

TULLY: For your information Tommy I...

ROWLEY: Did the provisionals threaten you Mr Tully...

TULLY: I know nothing and I'm saying nothing...

ROWLEY: ...or did they help you to squat here in return for favours?

TULLY: ...and you understand nothing.

ROWLEY: You've been unlucky I'd say. Someone mixed up his Donovans.

BIFFO: Petrol bomb...

NOBBY: Look out...

[*A petrol bomb crashes through the window and flares up in the room.*]

ROWLEY: Smother it.

TULLY: Those are my bed clothes.

NOBBY: Fucking hell...

ROWLEY: Very cool, lads, well done...

[*The bomb is smothered out.*]

Will you go and ask them to stop?

TULLY: I will not.

ROWLEY: You'll be burned with us.

TULLY: Fuck off.

BIFFO: The vehicles are coming sir.

ROWLEY: Who's got the gas gun?

BIFFO: Sergeant Cooper upstairs.

ROWLEY: Right...

[*ROWLEY goes upstairs.*]

NOBBY: Well, it's a fucking shambles again.

TULLY: For your information Tommy – Nineteen
Seventeen I was a stretcher bearer. RAMC.

NOBBY: Rob all my comrades.

TULLY: Fucking Western Front. You know nothing...
They know nothing Michael... They're just wee lads.

[*ROWLEY reappears with a loud hailer.*]

ROWLEY: If you do not... [*The hailer isn't working.*] ...

NOBBY: Turn the nob up.

WILLIAMS: Don't be filthy.

ROWLEY: Thank you...

TULLY: Come home, what happens? Nineteen Twenty.
All Catholics thrown out of the ship yards.

NOBBY: It's bloody fifty years ago...

TULLY: They're just boys Michael.

ROWLEY: If you do not... That's better... Please
disperse. If you do not disperse we shall use special
weapons... [*Turns away from hailer to people in the room.*]
When I say go, walk very calmly to the vehicles... [*On
hailer again.*] ... Thank you Sergeant Cooper...

[*We hear the bang-bang-bang of the gas gun and the cries
of the crowd.*]

TULLY: What is this? Gas?

ROWLEY: Right. That's made them spew a bit. Off we go now lads.

[*They all go except MICHAEL DONOVAN who is left sitting bewildered on his mattress. Outside we hear the crowd and dustbin lids and vehicles revving.*]

DONOVAN: ... [*Questioning noise.*] ...

[*Then WILLIAMS and BIFFO burst back into the room.*]

WILLIAMS: For Christ's sake lad you were in charge of him.

BIFFO: I was at the window.

WILLIAMS: Before that you were in charge.

BIFFO: I was sent upstairs.

WILLIAMS: You've got to think in the army, you know, just like everywhere else.

BIFFO: I know.

WILLIAMS: Come on granddad.

DONOVAN: ... [*Noise.*] ...

WILLIAMS: I said come on.

BIFFO: He can't hear you.

WILLIAMS: Oh Jesus...

BIFFO: Try shouting.

WILLIAMS: Stand up you stupid old potato.

BIFFO: No effect.

WILLIAMS: Carry him... One two hup...

[*They lift DONOVAN into an improvised seat of their linked hands.*]

DONOVAN: ... [*Noise.*] ...

WILLIAMS: He's bloody heavy.

BIFFO: D'you think he was in the Irish Guards?

WILLIAMS: Why not? It took my uncle the same way you know.

BIFFO: The army?

WILLIAMS: Thrombosis.

BIFFO: Oh...

WILLIAMS: Yes. On a fine day they used to sit him outside at the bus-stop.

DONOVAN: ... [*Noise.*] ...

WILLIAMS: Don't worry granddad. You'll be tortured and then dumped outside the Catholic hospital...

SCENE FOUR

BLOODY AWFUL COUNTRY

The bunkhouse which 'B' platoon shares with HQ platoon, is in a converted classroom of the infants school. Pin-ups, etc. Bunks. Crowded. Windows blocked out by coloured paper or big drawings of fairyland people and animals.

[Corporal WILLIAMS is fully kitted-up and playing cards with THISTLE who is stripped to the waist. NOBBY and BIFFO are in the process of kitting up. There is another soldier asleep in his bunk.]

NOBBY: Roll me over in the clover, roll me over, lay me down and... by the way, Biffo.

BIFFO: Hello.

NOBBY: Didn't you say while we was having our dinner that you've got something to bring to the notice of our old pal, Corporal Williams?

BIFFO: Oh ay. So I did.

WILLIAMS: Two bloody aces.

NOBBY: You what?

THISTLE: Two aces.

WILLIAMS: He's done it again. Two bloody aces.

BIFFO: Never.

WILLIAMS: He's cheating.

THISTLE: I'm not you know.

NOBBY: You're famous for it.

THISTLE: How is it, then, that I'm stripped to the bloody waist?

WILLIAMS: Because you fancy me.

BIFFO: His nipples are funny, though, aren't they?

THISTLE: Shut up. I'm stripped to the bloody waist so as to make clear even to you that I've nothing up my sleeves.

WILLIAMS: Marked pack.

THISTLE: Eh?

WILLIAMS: Marked bloody pack.

NOBBY: Not for the first time.

BIFFO: Stripping off's a diversion.

NOBBY: Course it is.

THISTLE: If you look closely you'll see that the cards belong to my opponent.

WILLIAMS: Naturally.

NOBBY: That's the cunning of it.

BIFFO: Who's got my bloody flak-jacket?

SLEEPING SOLDIER: [*Waking, shouting.*] ...Why don't
you sods shut up?

ALL: [*Cheers.*] ...

WILLIAMS: Fucking rude some people aren't they?

NOBBY: Shouting their heads off in the billet.

SLEEPING SOLDIER: ...Shut up...

WILLIAMS: Is he trying to sleep?

NOBBY: Roll me over, in the...

THISTLE: Another shuffle?

WILLIAMS: I'm not playing you if you win.

NOBBY: Referring to what I was saying about having
something to mention to you... is the officer coming
with us on this patrol?

WILLIAMS: Er – how d'you mean Nobby?

THISTLE: How d'you think I mean?

WILLIAMS: Thistle, I actually mentioned these two in a
letter to my wife. There are two young soldiers in my
section who give me a good laugh, but unhappily they
have evil minds.

NOBBY: No, I haven't. The army's made a man of me.

BIFFO: Seriously. Is it across the interface?

WILLIAMS: Seriously? Is what across the interface?

BIFFO: The patrol...

WILLIAMS: Oh. The patrol...

NOBBY: Yes. The patrol. Don't throw that king away.

WILLIAMS: Don't tell him I've got it will you?

THISTLE: Thank you very much, Nobby.

WILLIAMS: Come on. Get kitted up.

BIFFO: Is it?

WILLIAMS: Wait and see.

NOBBY: Because if it is across the interface and into the Protestant district the fact is...

WILLIAMS: I know your bloody facts.

NOBBY: Not this one you don't.

BIFFO: Fifty One Donegal Avenue.

WILLIAMS: Eh?

NOBBY: Tell him.

WILLIAMS: Tell me what?

NOBBY: Woman who lives there. Big blonde with two daughters.

BIFFO: You saw her at the dance.

WILLIAMS: Dance?

NOBBY: The Community Relations Dance.

THISTLE: You said there were dozens of women.

WILLIAMS: All horrible. I came home early.

THISTLE: I remember.

BIFFO: This one's not horrible.

NOBBY: She fancies you like bloody mad.

BIFFO: And what's more...

NOBBY: Her husband's at work all day.

BIFFO: Electricity Board.

THISTLE: ... [*Laughter.*] ...

WILLIAMS: Donegal Avenue?

BIFFO: Yes.

WILLIAMS: And she fancies me?

NOBBY: Yes.

WILLIAMS: I don't believe you.

NOBBY: She can't wait for it.

WILLIAMS: If it's me she fancies how come it's you two that know?

BIFFO: She told us.

WILLIAMS: It's you and the daughters isn't it? That's the real scene.

BIFFO: She saw you at the dance.

WILLIAMS: All right then, what does she look like?

NOBBY: Big blonde woman. Red dress.

WILLIAMS: Red dress?

BIFFO: Yes.

WILLIAMS: Oh.

THISTLE: What d'you mean... oh...?

WILLIAMS: Well as a matter of fact I did notice a... Big woman?

NOBBY: Yes.

WILLIAMS: Big?

BIFFO: Yes.

NOBBY: We only need be in there five minutes.

WILLIAMS: You mean leave the vehicle?

NOBBY: I mean use your initiative.

THISTLE: Knock on the door...

NOBBY: Quick stand-up job.

THISTLE: Hand on your zip and you're out.

WILLIAMS: Does she really fancy me?

NOBBY: I've told you...

WILLIAMS: ... [*Weighing it.*] ...

NOBBY: On the other hand, Thistle, he can't just knock on the door can he? I mean, that's blatant...

WILLIAMS: Listen. I bloody know how it's done.

THISTLE: Course you do.

WILLIAM: Park the vehicle outside. Inspect the licences in the windows of a few cars...

NOBBY: ...and if the lady of the house is in...

WILLIAMS: She'll pop out of the front door with an invitation to tea and bikkies. You must think I was born yesterday.

BIFFO: No we don't.

NOBBY: We don't: we remember you going over that fat woman in the Falls Road.

WILLIAMS: That was eighteen months ago.

THISTLE: Previous tour of duty.

BIFFO: And she was a Catholic like me.

WILLIAMS: Just shows how politics can change, don't it? Come on.

[*But before WILLIAMS can lead the section out CAPTAIN ROWLEY enters with JULIAN MASSINGHAM MP who has PPS rank in the Ministry.*]

ROWLEY: Before you go lads, let me introduce Mr Massingham from London: he's the Minister's PPS. His secretary...

MASSINGHAM: Hello...

WILLIAMS: Afternoon sir.

ROWLEY: Mr Massingham's brief is to report back on your living conditions.

MASSINGHAM: This room seems unusually crowded.

WILLIAMS: We're sharing sir. Our own billet was blown up.

MASSINGHAM: You were telling me...

ROWLEY: Yes.

MASSINGHAM: Food alright? Pin tables? Ping pong? Any other games equipment you'd like but don't have?

NOBBY: Yes.

MASSINGHAM: What's that?

NOBBY: A bit of cunt, sir.

ALL: ... [*Laughter.*] ...

SLEEPING SOLDIER: Why can't you shut up...?

ALL: ... [*Laughter.*] ...

MASSINGHAM: It is statistically true isn't it that so many Belfast men emigrate that the women out-number those who stay by five to one?

ROWLEY: So they say.

NOBBY: Easiest fuck in the UK.

MASSINGHAM: What?

NOBBY: We're forbidden to leave the post, sir. IRA.

MASSINGHAM: Security?

ROWLEY: Safety.

WILLIAMS: We have a discotheque at Battalion HQ.

ROWLEY: Girls come in for Community Dances.

MASSINGHAM: But for the rest you're cooped up here?

NOBBY: Some prefer it of course.

THISTLE: I do.

NOBBY: I know.

THISTLE: It's because I'm a pervert...

WILLIAMS: You what?

THISTLE: ...and what's more I can get on with my wood carving.

ALL: ... [*Groans.*] ...

MASSINGHAM: You're in marvellous spirits. People at home have no idea what it's like to face these thugs. They can be proud of you.

WILLIAMS: We just do our best.

ROWLEY: Off you go then.

WILLIAMS: Yes, sir.

ROWLEY: Across the interface?

WILLIAMS: Yes, sir.

ROWLEY: No stopping.

WILLIAMS: No, sir.

ROWLEY: Keep the vehicle moving.

WILLIAMS: Yes, sir.

NOBBY: Cheerio, sir.

MASSINGHAM: Cheerio. Good luck.

[*WILLIAMS, NOBBY and BIFFO go off to their patrol. THISTLE is ready for a wash.*]

THISTLE: Excuse me sir, if you don't mind.

ROWLEY: Carry on.

[*THISTLE gets his soap and goes. MASSINGHAM is peering out of the window.*]

MASSINGHAM: These blocks of flats are empty.

ROWLEY: They're the overshoot.

MASSINGHAM: What's the black flag?

ROWLEY: It's where we killed one of their snipers.

MASSINGHAM: Do they still get up there?

ROWLEY: Not much. We set parachute flares on trip wires.

MASSINGHAM: Where are the nearest Protestants?

ROWLEY: Beyond that ridge.

MASSINGHAM: It really is a bloody awful country isn't it?

ROWLEY: Yes.

MASSINGHAM: Have you met any of these Stormont people?

ROWLEY: Not really.

MASSINGHAM: Dreadful.

ROWLEY: Are they?

MASSINGHAM: Oh, their minds are as prehistoric as...

[*MASSINGHAM stops because he realises that the sleeping soldier could be awake and listening.*]

...Well... what was it like when you were blown up?

ROWLEY: Oh...

MASSINGHAM: I'm sorry. If you don't want to talk about it...

ROWLEY: I only remember one thing before the hospital.

MASSINGHAM: What was that?

ROWLEY: The blast.

MASSINGHAM: Oh...

ROWLEY: It took my breath. It was like... well actually it was like having a girl...

MASSINGHAM: A girl?

ROWLEY: Yes. The instant before you both come off.

MASSINGHAM: Heavens...

ROWLEY: Mm... D'you fancy a spin in an armoured car?

MASSINGHAM: Will they shoot at us?

ROWLEY: No.

MASSINGHAM: Oh.

ROWLEY: But it is nearly four o'clock, so if we pass the Secondary School they'll throw stones at us.

MASSINGHAM: Super. Let's go.

[*They go.*]

SCENE FIVE

A TURN FOR THE ARMY

Number Fifty One Donegall Avenue is a modern council house and we are in the hideously new and garish lounge.

[*MRS BRADY is at the frilly curtains looking out.*]

MRS BRADY: Brenda, will you come here? Will you come quick girl?

BRENDA: What's up?

[*BRENDA is about seventeen.*]

MRS BRADY: Look.

BRENDA: Soldiers.

MRS BRADY: Look again.

BRENDA: What are they doing?

MRS BRADY: Checking car licences.

BRENDA: Those cars are in the same place every day.

MRS BRADY: Sure. Put the kettle on.

BRENDA: What?

MRS BRADY: Do as you're told.

[*BRENDA goes.*]

Do you not see who it is?

BRENDA: [*From the kitchen.*] Who?

MRS BRADY: It's my Corporal.

BRENDA: [*Reappearing.*] ...Yours?

MRS BRADY: My God, there's Mrs Campbell. She's on her doorstep. She's going to invite them first.

[*MRS BRADY rushes to the door then stops.*]

No. You go. If Mrs Campbell sees me she'll take the wrong idea and gossip.

BRENDA: I'm in my slippers.

MRS BRADY: Brenda...

BRENDA: My legs look dreadful in slippers.

MRS BRADY: Will you make a fool of me?

BRENDA: Then ask them in.

[*BRENDA is peeved, but she has to go. MRS BRADY watches.*]

MRS BRADY: My God. Will you look at that brazen Campbell woman. She's seen Brenda. She's stepping forward herself. Brenda... Brenda's seen her. Run Brenda... That's my girlie. Mrs Campbell's running. Turn around soldier. He has done. He's seen Brenda. They're coming here. Thank God... my breath is all of a flutter... Oh, hell it's that flatulence. Whenever I get a chance of it with another man I get this damned flatulence... Kettle. Best china and biscuits... Too late.

[*Enter CORPORAL WILLIAMS followed by NOBBY, BIFFO and BRENDA. The soldiers are in battle uniform with guns and flak jackets.*]

Well, hello there. How many teas is it boys?

NOBBY: Three.

MRS BRADY: No coffee?

WILLIAMS: Er...

MRS BRADY: Wasn't it you at the Community Dance?

WILLIAMS: Er... me?

MRS BRADY: Will the boys outside take tea?

NOBBY: They'll take the lead off your roof.

WILLIAMS: This is very kind of you, Mrs...

MRS BRADY: Sit down. Kettle's on. Call me Babs. You're a shy one but it was you sung the song at the dance wasn't it? I thought you were great. Didn't I Brenda? I really thought you were great.

NOBBY: What did we tell you?

WILLIAMS: Shut up.

MRS BRADY: Did you see that in the paper about the Catholic women?

WILLIAMS: Er... we only read the sport.

MRS BRADY: Telling their children where to throw petrol bombs. How can women behave like that? Jungle beasts. Is the kettle boiled Brenda?

BRENDA: I'll see.

BIFFO: I'll go with you.

WILLIAMS: It is him fancies the daughter.

NOBBY: Shut up.

[BIFFO and BRENDA go to the kitchen.]

MRS BRADY: Will you take a sweet biscuit? You were just great at the dance... I mean we're British. There's a lower standard of life in the Republic. Or d'you like cream wafers? There's no social services and no – well, there's no contraception.

NOBBY: Now there's a subject that interests the Corporal.

MRS BRADY: Subject?

NOBBY: Contraception.

MRS BRADY: Is that a fact?

WILLIAMS: You could say so, yes...

MRS BRADY: Well that's great. Isn't that great?

NOBBY: Excuse me...

[*NOBBY goes into the kitchen. Moment of embarrassment.*]

MRS BRADY: Er... have you looked at the map?

WILLIAMS: Map?

MRS BRADY: The Roman Catholics live in a ring round the city. That's deliberate so that we can't reach the docks.

WILLIAMS: Er... That girl can't be your daughter.

MRS BRADY: Do you wonder that in our opinion the army's doing a grand job?

WILLIAMS: You're too sexy to have a daughter that old.

MRS BRADY: Fucking kiss me.

[*Attempt at a passionate kiss but his gear gets in the way.*]

WILLIAMS: Hang on. It's my accoutrements.

MRS BRADY: You're deeply shy aren't you?

WILLIAMS: Well...

MRS BRADY: I knew you would be.

[*Another embrace, but this time NOBBY, BIFFO and BRENDA return.*]

NOBBY: Been examining her vehicle licence?

WILLIAMS: Shut up.

BRENDA: D'you all want sugar?

MRS BRADY: Damned flatulence... Are you good at electricals?

NOBBY: She has a plug upstairs.

WILLIAMS: A what?

MRS BRADY: Well actually it's a socket.

WILLIAMS: A socket?

MRS BRADY: It needs looking at.

WILLIAMS: Why not? I'll have my tea when I come down.

MRS BRADY: That's great. Odd job man. Isn't that great Brenda? Damned flatulence.

[*MRS BRADY and WILLIAMS go upstairs.*]

BRENDA: Will the boys outside take sugar?

NOBBY: If you just give me the mugs, Brenda, I know when I'm not wanted...

[*BRENDA pours. Ready. BIFFO is a little apart.*]

NOBBY: Have you told your mum he's a Catholic?

BRENDA: He's not as handsome as you is he?

BIFFO: Nothing like.

[*BIFFO opens the door for NOBBY.*]

NOBBY: I'll give you ten minutes.

[*NOBBY goes. BRENDA and BIFFO are finally alone.*]

BIFFO: Well... we've never really been alone like this have we?

BRENDA: No.

BIFFO: I mean there's so much to say isn't there?

BRENDA: Is there?

BIFFO: Yes.

BRENDA: What?

BIFFO: Well... Oh, I say, I like that picture...

BRENDA: Mum bought it in Austria.

BIFFO: Austria?

BRENDA: It was on a coach tour.

BIFFO: Oh... er... what is it?

BRENDA: What?

BIFFO: The picture.

BRENDA: Who cares what... wood carving. I don't know. I didn't go with them that year. It was my first holiday with my pals. Butlins. You should see the ballrooms.

BIFFO: Your first holiday.

BRENDA: My only one...

BIFFO: Oh...

BRENDA: So far...

BIFFO: Oh, Brenda...

[*BIFFO goes to her and kisses her.*]

BRENDA: Oh, Biffo. I do love you.

BIFFO: I... [*Disengages, wants to speak his mind.*] What I want to say Brenda is that the reason I joined the army... well the reason was that my girlfriend gave me the push.

BRENDA: Great...

BIFFO: I know it sounds daft.

BRENDA: Thank you very much.

BIFFO: Listen Brenda. It's important. When I left school I had a job. Packer in a warehouse.

BRENDA: ... [*A little snort of disdain.*] ...

BIFFO: I know, it was nothing. Then I got laid off. I tried for another job but I couldn't find one. I mean, I've no certificates or what have you. After a bit I stopped trying, which was when Sharon said...

BRENDA: Sharon?

BIFFO: My girlfriend.

BRENDA: Are you engaged?

BIFFO: She gave me the push. I thought sod it and joined the army and the point is...

BRENDA: You still love her.

BIFFO: No. But in all fairness Brenda I must tell you that I'll not find a better job in civvy street so I should stay in the army whatever happens.

BRENDA: Whatever happens?

BIFFO: Yes.

BRENDA: You mean there's other girls?

BIFFO: Other girls? What other girls?

BRENDA: ... [*A huge sniff and sob.*] ...

BIFFO: Oh come on Brenda. This isn't just a quick stand up job like your mother and the Corporal.

BRENDA: My mother's beautiful.

BIFFO: Don't cry.

BRENDA: ... [*Boo-hooing.*] ...

BIFFO: What I mean is that since Sharon I've become more of a man...

BRENDA: Oh...

BIFFO: This is ridiculous.

[*BRENDA... still boo-hooing.*]

BIFFO: Close your eyes.

BRENDA: I will not.

BIFFO: Close your bloody eyes.

> [*BRENDA screws up her face and turns it away, but she does close her eyes. BIFFO kisses her... very gently.*]

BRENDA: Oh... [*Opens her eyes.*] Oh Biffo...

BIFFO: I think it's you Brenda.

BRENDA: I know it's you Biffo.

BIFFO: That's what I mean, you see I...

BRENDA: ... [*Giggles.*] ...

BIFFO: This is serious. I'm asking you to bloody marry me...

BRENDA: ... [*Silent, waiting.*] ...

BIFFO: Then something turns sick in my stomach, and I remember I'm Catholic...

BRENDA: My best friend at work is Catholic.

BIFFO: Is she?

BRENDA: You don't care about it?

BIFFO: No.

BRENDA: Would I have to turn?

BIFFO: Not for me.

BRENDA: What about...?

BIFFO: What about what...?

BRENDA: The children.

BIFFO: Oh. Er... well in England there's more choice isn't there?

BRENDA: Is there?

BIFFO: I think so.

BRENDA: Oh.

BIFFO: Er... are you giving me your answer?

BRENDA: ...They don't really put marks on the soles of their feet, do they?

BIFFO: Eh?

BRENDA: Priests.

BIFFO: Priests?

BRENDA: They don't go into hospital and put marks on the new born babies feet...

BIFFO: Oh bloody hell Brenda, how daft can you get?

BRENDA: I know it's daft.

BIFFO: Then why d'you believe it?

BRENDA: I don't believe it.

BIFFO: Then why ask me?

BRENDA: Because... Biffo. Hold me.

[*Embrace. Then knocking and shouting at the front door.*]

NOBBY: [*Outside.*] ...Biffo. Corporal. Come on. Come on lads.

BRENDA: What's that?

BIFFO: Something's happened...

[*BIFFO lets NOBBY in.*]

BIFFO: What is it?

NOBBY: On the Catholic side. Come on. Ops. Room are going bloody mad.

[*NOBBY leaves the front room to shout upstairs.*]

Come on. Unplug yourselves. Come on.

BIFFO: But what's happened?

BRENDA: Biffo.

BIFFO: Eh?

BRENDA: It's yes.

BIFFO: What's yes?

NOBBY: [*Off.*] It's a bloody alert.

BRENDA: The answer to the question.

BIFFO: What question, you... [*Then he realises.*] ...Oh...

BRENDA: The answer's yes.

BIFFO: Oh, I say...

[*NOBBY reappears.*]

NOBBY: My God. Lovebirds.

[*Enter MRS BRADY followed by a deshabille WILLIAMS.*]

Hello. Did you get your socket mended?

WILLIAMS: Don't be bloody filthy to a woman.

NOBBY: But with her husband in the Electricity Board, I
    mean, who thought she'd need a service call?

WILLIAMS: Just say what happened.

NOBBY: They've set fire to the school bus.

WILLIAMS: Where?

NOBBY: Up the Murph.

WILLIAMS: It's bloody miles away.

MRS BRADY: Filthy Catholic savages.

NOBBY: Mr Rowley's there. He saw it all start.

WILLIAMS: What did you give as our position?

NOBBY: Top of Sten Gun Alley.

WILLIAMS: Woodvale Corner?

NOBBY: It gives us time.

WILLIAMS: He's right. Well done.

MRS BRADY: Will I see you again?

WILLIAMS: Of course you will, Blossom.

NOBBY: Blossom?

WILLIAMS: Get moving.

MRS BRADY: Will you see the boys to the door, Brenda. If Mrs Campbell sees me in this state she'll get the wrong idea.

[*BRENDA takes WILLIAMS, NOBBY and BIFFO to the door.*]

There she is. Behind the curtains. Watching. Mangy bitch. My God. Brenda's kissed that boy. There's surely nothing happened there. She was brought up to say no. Oh, God. There they go... Set fire to a school bus. What did my grandmother say? We may look the same as Roman Catholics and live in the same bloody awful poverty, but what makes us better is that we know when we've done wrong... Now what shall I tell Brenda? I know. He mended the socket while I changed my undies in the bathroom.

[*BRENDA returns with the empty mugs from outside.*]

Well that was obliging of the Corporal, to attend to the socket while I... It could upset your father, of course, him being electrical, but if a man lets these odd jobs pile up he can't complain when... What's funny? Why are you smiling?

BRENDA: Oh ma...

MRS BRADY: What?

BRENDA: Plugs and sockets...

MRS BRADY: What d'you mean?

BRENDA: At your age.

MRS BRADY: At my age? Let me tell you I...

BRENDA: ... [*Giggling.*] ...

MRS BRADY: You cheeky...

BRENDA: Plugs and...

MRS BRADY: ... [*Giggling.*] ...

BRENDA: ... [*Laughing.*] ...

MRS BRADY: ... [*Laughing, then...*] Oh Brenda...

BRENDA: What?

MRS BRADY: We shouldn't.

BRENDA: Shouldn't what?

MRS BRADY: [*Giggling, then...*] He had nice nails. Did
  you notice?

BRENDA: Yes.

MRS BRADY: ... [*Another little giggle.*] ...

BRENDA: I love Biffo.

MRS BRADY: What?

BRENDA: He's asked me to marry him. I've said yes.

MRS BRADY: You're below the age.

BRENDA: He's Roman Catholic.

MRS BRADY: That soldier? That wee boy?

BRENDA: Biffo.

MRS BRADY: You... Did you stay off work deliberate today? Was this planned? My God was this...

BRENDA: I love him.

MRS BRADY: Love?

BRENDA: I met him six times at the discotheque.

MRS BRADY: Discotheque. It's a room in a barracks.

BRENDA: It's got coloured lights.

MRS BRADY: Would an officer send his daughter there? Well would he?

BRENDA: ... [*Tears.*] ...

MRS BRADY: Are you up the skits?

BRENDA: No.

MRS BRADY: But you've let him in you?

BRENDA: I have not.

MRS BRADY: For why?

BRENDA: I love him. That's 'for why'.

MRS BRADY: ... [*Sobs.*] ...

BRENDA: Oh, don't you start.

MRS BRADY: My wee girlie. Do you mind that white frock with ribbons? You were seven years old.

BRENDA: I was eight.

MRS BRADY: Seven.

BRENDA: I was eight.

MRS BRADY: [*Tears.*] ...A Roman Catholic.

BRENDA: He's mine.

MRS BRADY: Has he touched you?

BRENDA: What d'you mean?

MRS BRADY: You know what I mean.

BRENDA: I don't.

MRS BRADY: The parts of your body.

BRENDA: Is that what worries you?

MRS BRADY: You're my little girl.

BRENDA: I still love you.

MRS BRADY: In the old house, before the council moved us, and the old tin bath in from of the fire... I'd see you in it. So white. You were so thin, Brenda... have you a dry hanky?

BRENDA: ... [*Hands hanky.*] ...

MRS BRADY... [*Blows nose.*] ...

BRENDA: ... [*Takes back hanky.*] ...

MRS BRADY: A Roman Catholic.

BRENDA: Yes.

MRS BRADY: They say a lot of the military are, especially the Scots.

BRENDA: Yes.

MRS BRADY: He's a very shy boy.

BRENDA: Yes.

MRS BRADY: I like that.

BRENDA: I know you do... [*Looking out of window.*] Oh God.

MRS BRADY: What?

BRENDA: Here's my father.

MRS BRADY: He's a selfish fool.

BRENDA: Will you help me?

MRS BRADY: It goes hard Brenda.

BRENDA: Will you help me?

[*Enter MR BRADY. Donkey-jacketed from work.*]

BRADY: Hello there. How's your sore throat?

BRENDA: OK Dad.

BRADY: Is that tea for me?

BRENDA: It's cold.

BRADY: You're in your knickers.

MRS BRADY: I've the needle and thread to my dress.

BRADY: Who did drink the tea?

MRS BRADY: The military.

BRENDA: A patrol.

BRADY: I suppose they know my house...

MRS BRADY: They do. Alec Brady that's in the Vigilantes.

BRADY: Ay. They've seen me on the barricade at night.

[*BRADY goes.*]

MRS BRADY: Has he gone for his piss now?

BRENDA: Oh, ma...

MRS BRADY: Never said how I looked did he?

BRENDA: You look great.

MRS BRADY: I should have tea for him. It should be
    ready when he comes in. That's how his mother was,
    and his grandmother before that.

[*Enter BRADY. He has just taken his jacket and shoes off.*]

BRADY: We were in a house today – Roman Catholic bookmakers on the Malone Road – they called us to fix a fluorescent tube in a fish tank. More money than sense and the woman was blatant. She was forty minutes on the telephone. I said to Harry McGibbon who was with me, I said my mother never entered a public house for a drink. My mother was a clean woman and much respected.

[*MRS BRADY allows a silence. Then...*]

MRS BRADY: Are you listening, Alec?

BRADY: Am I what?

MRS BRADY: One of the British soldiers has asked Brenda to marry him...

[*BRADY looks up from MRS BRADY to BRENDA and back.*]

BRENDA: His name's Biffo.

BRADY: Biffo?

MRS BRADY: She's not pregnant, Alec.

BRADY: Then why look sick?

BRENDA: He's Roman Catholic.

BRADY: If this is a joke it's a very poor one.

BRENDA: It's no joke, I love him.

BRADY: What's your opinion? Did you not tell him she's under age?

MRS BRADY: How old was I when I married you?

BRADY: What's that got to do with it?

MRS BRADY: Alec, he's a very polite shy boy.

BRADY: So's the Pope.

BRENDA: I knew you'd say "no" because you hate Roman Catholics but he's an Englishman and his best friend was blown up and killed.

[*Silence. BRENDA sniffles.*]

BRADY: Is Margaret home from school?

MRS BRADY: No.

BRADY: Have you seen her science notebook? The neatness: what a treat.

BRENDA: You love Margaret more than me.

BRADY: I what?

BRENDA: You always have done.

BRADY: Brenda, you're a fool we all know that but for your information I don't hate any man because he's a Roman Catholic.

BRENDA: You do dad.

BRADY: I don't hate any man, Brenda. I hope I'm more humble than that. What I do say is that the Constitution must not be overthrown.

BRENDA: ... [*Questioning look.*] ...

MRS BRADY: ... [*Sits quiet.*] ...

BRADY: ... [*Silence.*] ...

BRENDA: What does that mean, dad, exactly?

BRADY: You can marry who the hell you choose.

BRENDA: I need your consent.

BRADY: You can ask a magistrate.

BRENDA: I don't want to.

BRADY: I'll be mocked by no girl, I'll tell you.

[*BRADY gets up.*]

I'm having a sleep. It's my watch tonight.

[*BRADY goes.*]

BRENDA: But I want him to help me.

MRS BRADY: Is there no one else you fancy?

BRENDA: I've been a good girl.

[*MRS BRADY looks. Then picks up the tea things and takes them out.*]

Oh damn... I'll help you dry.

SCENE SIX

MUG SHOTS

SUSAN DOHERTY is six years old and a totally immobile and bandaged figure in a cot bed in the Catholic Hospital. One of her limbs is held up by a pulley and she has a bottle for her urine and a drip feed. There is a chair at her bedside and two more in the body of the ward.

[*SISTER WALLACE leads FATHER TOM BOGAN who is really about 40 but looks older. She has just opportunistically nabbed him in the corridor outside.*]

BOGAN: Sister Wallace you're an absolute menace of a woman. I've no-one to visit in your ward.

SISTER: Very lucky I saw you passing.

BOGAN: I've an old man in the upstairs geriatrics.

SISTER: Now where's that snuggly gingerbread girl Susan Doherty and who's come all this way to see her? Father Tom Bogan from St Stephen Martyr...

BOGAN: I don't know any Susan...

[*BOGAN looks down into the cot and sees SUSAN.*]

SISTER: Blink your eyes Susan.

[*SUSAN blinks.*]

Susan can't move her gingerbread jaw, you see, so she speaks by blinking.

BOGAN: Well hello there, Susan: that's just fine...

SISTER: Your mam can't come today Susan so Father Bogan says he'll read your new comic.

BOGAN: I can't... [*Doesn't want to argue in front of SUSAN, so he walks apart. SISTER WALLACE follows him.*]

Sister I've to see the old man and then I've a meeting and the confessions...

SISTER: Help me out.

BOGAN: Where's your staff?

SISTER: There's two off with flu.

BOGAN: I must be on time for my meeting.

SISTER: Susan was blown up in Brewery Street. Her dad and her sister were killed.

BOGAN: That's blackmail.

SISTER: I did you a favour over the boy that cut his thumb off: now don't you owe me one?

BOGAN: You're a blasted schemer.

SISTER: I'm sure Susan could speak a little but she won't because her mother never visits.

BOGAN: Why not?

SISTER: Och, she'd left the husband anyway. Now

here's your chair and here's your comic.

BOGAN: Have you spoken to her parish priest?

SISTER: Of course we've – what's wrong?

BOGAN: Which story does she want?

SISTER: That one.

BOGAN: That's outrageous even for you.

SISTER: Just close your mind and read it. Susan loves that character, come what may.

BOGAN: I can't read...

SISTER: It's Whacky, Susan. Very naughty, isn't he, but we know he doesn't really mean it.

[*SISTER goes before FATHER BOGAN can haggle any more, so he is left holding the comic.*]

BOGAN: Well, er... Susan... Whacky, it says because he's always getting whacked. Whacky offers to clean the car but ends up polishing it off. Shall I describe each picture and read what it says? Here's Whacky then in his little red sweater and short pants and he says: "Shall I clean the car for you dad, please?" Whacky's dad: "Hum, well, I suppose so. But be careful. I don't want to end up whacking you." Second picture. Whacky has the hosepipe going and he says: "Easy does it. Mustn't make dad cross by splashing the seats". That's a thing I should have told you Susan. The car has no top on it. It's what they call a two seater. D'you understand?

[*SUSAN blinks.*]

That's very good that blinking. Was it Sister Wallace's idea?

[*SUSAN blinks.*]

BOGAN [*Continued*]: No surprise. Third picture. Whacky
    says: "I'd better clean out the exhaust pipe, too, it's got
    soot in it", and there he goes, shoving the hosepipe up
    the exhaust. He's like a serving boy I knew who came
    to the altar with a live mouse in his pocket. Fourth
    picture. Whacky's dad says "My car" exclamation mark
    and Whacky says "Crikey" exclamation mark "I've
    done it again" and the car – well the entire shebang's
    burst open with water. There's water entering through
    the exhaust, Susan, it shoots out of both headlamps and
    the bonnet's way up and all the bits of the engine are
    flying through the air. Boom, it says. Clatter. Whiz.
    Sploosh. I'll tell you a good word when I used to read
    comics. Yaronck. Can you say it? Yaronck...

[*BOGAN glances at SUSAN.*]

Very nearly. After you've said your prayers practice
Yaronck. Next picture. "Bother", says Whacky, "don't
worry dad. I'll close the bonnet" and his dad stands
with his arms very rigid by his side and his mouth
open and coming out of his mouth are the letters that
make up the word "Speechless". As well he might be.
I'm rushing through now Susan because I've an old
man upstairs to see. Shall I send him your love? I will.
Well... Whacky closes the bonnet but being Whacky
he traps the hose in it and so here it says Whack. Biff.
Bonk. Trash. Yaronck. My Gosh. They still use
Yaronck... "Turn off the water, dad, I'm being
whacked with the hose". "Just what you deserve" says
dad, but in the next picture it says in capital letters
SWELL exclamation mark, because the hosepipe has
swelled up with water like a giant sausage and there's
Whacky trying not to roll off the top of it and at the
side his dad with his hands over his ears because he
knows what to expect and there it is Susan, in big red
letters it says Bang exclamation mark (do you know
what I mean when I say exclamation mark?) and

Whacky says "Yaroooww" with three letter os and two letter ws and... Susan? What's wrong Susan? Are you OK?... Sorry my mistake. You're just having a wee smile.

[*SISTER WALLACE enters followed by ROWLEY and FOSTER.*]

SISTER: Wait here please.

ROWLEY: Thank you.

[*SISTER WALLACE leaves ROWLEY and FOSTER by the two chairs. They have a bunch of flowers and she has a hypodermic on a sterilised tray.*]

SISTER: So is that all fine then Father Bogan?

BOGAN: It is.

SISTER: Did you finish the story Susan?

BOGAN: Well, no Sister, I...

SISTER: I'll tell you what. I'll finish it later myself.

BOGAN: Fine.

SISTER: Isn't she a brave gingerbread girl?

BOGAN: She is: and I'm sure she says her prayers to herself: I'll be away now to the geriatrics...

SISTER: Of course we had all that out with Monsignor Rourke two years ago.

BOGAN: All what?

SISTER: Comics and TV in the ward.

BOGAN: Oh.

SISTER: What was good for the children and what was not. Nothing decided of course. The Monsignor's an old woman.

BOGAN: Sister, if you must say that...

SISTER: Say it in the privacy of my office.

BOGAN: Aye. So I'll say cheerio now and...

[*Injection finished.*]

SISTER: Father: won't you offer a wee prayer?

[*In all conscience FATHER BOGAN cannot refuse. They bow in prayer. Our attention turns to the waiting ROWLEY and FOSTER.*]

ROWLEY: Oh my God...

FOSTER: What's the matter?

ROWLEY: Now they're chewing the rosary...

FOSTER: At least we can chat in private.

ROWLEY: What?

FOSTER: You've been avoiding me haven't you?

ROWLEY: No.

FOSTER: That didn't sound too convincing.

ROWLEY: It was a bloody stupid question.

FOSTER: Oh I don't blame you Mike. I know how Marion can embarrass people.

ROWLEY: ... [*No reply, wanting to close that particular subject.*]

FOSTER: She can do it very well when she tries.

ROWLEY: Geoff, let it go...

FOSTER: So she has been a nuisance to Sheila.

ROWLEY: A nuisance?

FOSTER: You know what I mean.

ROWLEY: I don't.

FOSTER: Whenever I telephone Marion she's practically hysterical. She can't cope on her own. I really must apply for a permanent UK posting...

ROWLEY: Well if that's what you want to do...

FOSTER: I don't really know what I want. Has she pestered Sheila?

ROWLEY: No.

FOSTER: Can I believe that?

ROWLEY: ... [*No reply.*] ...

FOSTER: I'm sorry.

ROWLEY: What about?

FOSTER: Our friendship.

ROWLEY: We've still got it.

FOSTER: Have we?

ROWLEY: Oh shut up. Geoff.

[*Silence.*]

BOGAN: Amen...

[*The prayers are finished. SISTER WALLACE and BOGAN face the two officers.*]

SISTER: Well. Susan's flooded with visitors today. Do you know Father Bogan?

BOGAN: Hello there.

ROWLEY: Mike Rowley

FOSTER: Geoffrey Foster.

BOGAN: If you can excuse me gentlemen...

ROWLEY: Don't I know you by sight?

BOGAN: Er – are you billeted in the infants' school?

ROWLEY: Yes.

BOGAN: That's it then. Now I have a wee visit to an old man upstairs, brought in by your people as a matter of fact.

ROWLEY: Not Michael Donovan?

BOGAN: You know him? Poor soul.

ROWLEY: We interned his mate Billy Tully.

BOGAN: I know. Old Billy. His solicitor came to the Aid Committee. Well cheerio now, Sister, and God bless.

SISTER: Thank you Father Bogan.

[*FATHER BOGAN has gone.*]

Och, that man's never on time. He does too many kindnesses on the way.

ROWLEY: Er... Geoffrey.

FOSTER: Sorry.

[*FOSTER hands SISTER WALLACE the flowers.*]

For Susan.

SISTER: Gracious. Aren't they just smashers?

FOSTER: The entire Brewery Street platoon chipped in for them.

SISTER: Very decent. What a pity that Susan can't see them.

ROWLEY: She can't see them?

SISTER: She's just now had her injection.

ROWLEY: What's that got to do with it?

SISTER: She'll sleep for three or four hours. Will you wait here while I fetch a vase?

[*SISTER WALLACE goes off with the flowers.*]

ROWLEY: Asleep... That bloody woman's on to us.

FOSTER: We've not done anything yet.

ROWLEY: She knows what we want. O Lord, have you seen the child's face?

FOSTER: She can't know what we want.

ROWLEY: Well she doesn't know we've got fifteen photographs of known IRA bomb men, but she's a fair idea that we've come to question Susan without anybody knowing. We hoped...

FOSTER: Proves the Colonel's point though doesn't it?

ROWLEY: What point?

FOSTER: Hospital. They either keep you out on medical grounds or let you come in knowing damn well that they'll find out more than you.

ROWLEY: Oh yes. They're everywhere you know.

FOSTER: Who?

ROWLEY: Fenians.

FOSTER: Oh shut up.

ROWLEY: Especially in spinsters who want to be boss.

[*SISTER WALLACE returns with the flowers in a vase.*]

SISTER: There. Aren't they just grand?

ROWLEY: Good.

SISTER: When she wakes up I'll give her one to smell. Will you have a cocoa in my office?

ROWLEY: Our adjutant was machine gunned, once, in a hospital in Cyprus.

SISTER: What does that mean?

ROWLEY: Nothing. We'd love a cocoa, wouldn't we Geoffrey?

[*SISTER WALLACE leads them off.*]

SCENE SEVEN

TODAY'S NUMBERS

B Platoon are once again in occupation of the post in Brewery Street, although it is not yet fully repaired.

[*BIFFO at the makeshift RT assembly is immersed in a newspaper. WILLIAMS is in a canvas chair and speculating upon future triumphs.*]

WILLIAMS: Biffo...

BIFFO: Uh?

WILLIAMS: What would you say: two big items such as a dishwasher and a proper automatic washing machine, or the washing machine plus two or three smaller items?

BIFFO: Er...

WILLIAMS: Say... a washing machine, a mixer, a sewing machine and a toaster and all that lot. Or on the third hand put everything into a massive hi-fi with extension speakers in bathroom and lavatory. No. That's a toy for me and our Doreen isn't it, and we have enough of that pop music as it is.

BIFFO: How old's Doreen?

WILLIAMS: Sixteen.

BIFFO: What about a colour TV?

WILLIAMS: No, no. It must be something helpful for the wife.

BIFFO: Then ask her.

WILLIAMS: But if you was me, Biffo, and you wanted to surprise her.

BIFFO: Oh if I was you there'd be a big piss up for the lads.

WILLIAMS: Look, I've told Nobby, you can put that out of your heads. A few friendly light ales, yes, but a big piss up...

[*The phone rings. BIFFO answers.*]

BIFFO: Ops. Room... Yes... You've given admittance?... You're a filthy homosexual...

[*BIFFO hangs up.*]

Sammy at the OP. Rowley's arrived.

WILLIAMS: Anybody with him?

BIFFO: Just a driver.

WILLIAMS: Don't half swan about do they? Where was I?

BIFFO: Hi-fi.

WILLIAMS: Yes. I'd like it.

BIFFO: Who wouldn't.

WILLIAMS: It should be for the wife, though, shouldn't it?

BIFFO: What about Brenda's mum?

WILLIAMS: Eh?

BIFFO: Brenda's mum.

WILLIAMS: She was a free fuck son. She should give me something.

BIFFO: I daresay, but you wouldn't half help me if you gave her a bottle of Cherry B.

WILLIAMS: Cherry brandy?

BIFFO: Yes.

WILLIAMS: For Brenda's mum?

BIFFO: She's on my side you see.

WILLIAMS: What's in it for me?

BIFFO: Well. She was.

WILLIAMS: Who told you to say that? Nobby?

BIFFO: Come on Corporal, it's my future happiness.

WILLIAMS: I'm very glad Biffo to see you settling down and I wish Nobby could do the same.

BIFFO: I must keep her mum on my side because Brenda's under age. It's a question of Brenda coming to the UK when we leave here and asking a magistrate.

WILLIAMS: Runaway lovers...

BIFFO: Well Brenda's running.

WILLIAMS: Has she said she will?

BIFFO: She's going to phone me.

WILLIAMS: And her mum's in on the plot?

BIFFO: Will you buy a bottle or not?

WILLIAMS: Does she like Cherry B?

BIFFO: Yes.

WILLIAMS: You're sure?

BIFFO: Yes.

WILLIAMS: Why can't she run off without help from her mother?

BIFFO: Will you buy it or not?

WILLIAMS: Who gives it to her?

BIFFO: You do.

WILLIAMS: The last patrol...

BIFFO: Don't take the piss Corporal.

WILLIAMS: I think that in the circumstances Biffo, we might run to a bottle of Cherry B.

BIFFO: Oh smashing. You see they're all having rows because Mr Brady's been told.

WILLIAMS: Eh?

BIFFO: She told him.

WILLIAMS: Not about me?

[*The phone rings. BIFFO answers.*]

BIFFO: Ops. Room... You what? Yes...

WILLIAMS: Does he know about me?

BIFFO: Ssh... I know but what happened was...

WILLIAMS: Listen, he's in the Vigilantes and they've handed out some right thrashings.

BIFFO: The number was out of order. No. We were blown up. Can you please...

WILLIAMS: If he does know you lads must stand by me.

BIFFO: Er... When were the Jocks in here?

WILLIAMS: Has she told him about me?

BIFFO: Eh?

WILLIAMS: Mrs Brady.

BIFFO: No. About me.

WILLIAMS: Oh well in that case...

BIFFO: When were the Jocks in here?

WILLIAMS: In this post?

BIFFO: Yes.

WILLIAMS: Before us.

BIFFO: Sorry, love, but the Jocks went home in the summer...

WILLIAMS: Who is that?

[*Enter ROWLEY and THISTLE. They are in their flak jackets and carry mugs of hot soup.*]

ROWLEY: Morning Corporal. How's the scene of the explosion? Cook's got the soup on downstairs.

WILLIAMS: They say we'll be back here to sleep on Monday.

ROWLEY: Then UK at the end of the week.

WILLIAMS: Yes sir.

ROWLEY: Tremendous. We happened to be passing so we thought we'd drop in for the numbers.

WILLIAMS: We're just hanging on for them sir.

BIFFO: Certainly. Of course... That's just what I was thinking myself. Yes... I mean if the Jocks have gone home, I thought what about our lads...?

WILLIAMS: Er... any news of Mr Foster's posting sir?

ROWLEY: I believe he's forwarded an application.

WILLIAMS: We thought cassettes for a leaving present.

ROWLEY: Very good.

WILLIAMS: You don't know what composers do you sir?

BIFFO: Hang on... What's your collar size?

WILLIAMS: Eh?

BIFFO: Your collar size.

WILLIAMS: Sixteen.

BIFFO: Thistle?

THISTLE: Fifteen and a half.

BIFFO: What about you Mr Rowley?

ROWLEY: Er...

WILLIAMS: Fifteen and a half?

ROWLEY: Yes.

WILLIAMS: Fifteen and a half.

BIFFO: That's two fifteens, two fifteen and a half and one sixteen... Oh... They can only do blue.

WILLIAMS: Take them.

BIFFO: Well, alright, if that's all you can...

ROWLEY: Take what?

WILLIAMS: Shirts. I think.

BIFFO: Right. Tomorrow lunch hour. Ask the lad at the OP for... OP... It's the scaffolding with camouflage nets on top. There's a lad in there called Sammy, you... You say you want Corporal Williams... Er, oh, well, our tour of duty ends next week... In the spring I suppose... Ta-ra.

[*BIFFO hangs up.*]

BIFFO: D'you know what she just said?

WILLIAMS: The woman at the shirt factory?

BIFFO: Yes.

WILLIAMS: Took a fancy to the Jocks and promised them a few shirts.

BIFFO: Yes. They're drip dry nylon, is that all right?

WILLIAMS: All right? You played it a treat son.

THISTLE: The Jocks must have fucked them.

ROWLEY: We get those shirts through the officers' mess.

WILLIAMS: How much?

ROWLEY: Ten per cent discount.

BIFFO: These are free.

THISTLE: The Jocks did fuck them.

ROWLEY: The shirts aren't stolen?

WILLIAMS: She just rang up...

BIFFO: She said they're very slightly imperfect.

THISTLE: Thank you very much.

WILLIAMS: I wouldn't handle stolen gear.

ROWLEY: You did in Borneo.

WILLIAMS: That was whisky.

BIFFO: Can I just tell you what she said?

WILLIAMS: Eh?

BIFFO: She said how long are you here and I said we're going home next week.

WILLIAMS: We heard.

BIFFO: So she said when will you be back and I said oh, in the spring, like. To which she said: well, she said, if I don't see you in the spring I'll see you on the mattress.

[*Laughter.*]

WILLIAMS: Fucking hell. They're desperate aren't they?

ROWLEY: Well it's a very awful place isn't it?

WILLIAMS: Heard what the lads call it?

ROWLEY: What?

WILLIAMS: Beldrag.

THISTLE: Beldrag...

WILLIAMS: Give me Aden every time.

THISTLE: Hear, hear.

ROWLEY: We certainly knew where we were.

THISTLE: Knew who the enemy was.

WILLIAMS: As soon as a black man popped up you shot his head off.

THISTLE: Remember Sergeant Walters on water patrol?

ROWLEY: Water patrol...

WILLIAMS: Aye he was a vicious old bastard.

THISTLE: Funny isn't it how you remember the ones who got killed?

WILLIAMS: That fair-haired lad in Cyprus.

THISTLE: Eric.

WILLIAMS: Tommy Harrop in the Canal Zone.

THISTLE: Aye. Tommy Harrop.

[*Enter NOBBY.*]

NOBBY: Morning all.

ROWLEY: Morning Nobby.

NOBBY: Hello sir.

ROWLEY: Called in for the numbers?

NOBBY: Nearly time isn't it?

BIFFO: Nearly.

NOBBY: How much is on today?

WILLIAMS: A hundred and seventy five.

THISTLE: Christ.

WILLIAMS: I reckon it's mine.

ROWLEY: You reckon it's yours?

WILLIAMS: I only need one number.

THISTLE: Which?

NOBBY: Seven...

WILLIAMS: Thank you.

ROWLEY: How long since there's been one?

WILLIAMS: Three weeks.

THISTLE: Christ...

WILLIAMS: Law of averages. It's mine. I'm buying the wife some appliances.

NOBBY: For her legs?

WILLIAMS: For the house, you daft bastard.

ROWLEY: Is it time yet?

BIFFO: I'll just turn it up sir.

[*BIFFO turns up the volume on brigade radio. Buzzing and pipping.*]

RADIO VOICE: ...a red Ford Zephyr which evaded a road block in Leeson Street...

NOBBY: We want it quiet for the next week don't we?

THISTLE: Aye.

NOBBY: A nice quiet changeover and then back home...

BIFFO: By the way Nobby.

NOBBY: What?

BIFFO: I've ordered you a free shirt.

NOBBY: Where from?

WILLIAMS: Some women rang up from the factory.

NOBBY: Desperate aren't they?

BIFFO: Drip dry nylon.

NOBBY: I can't wear it.

BIFFO: Why not?

NOBBY: Tender skin.

WILLIAMS: Tender skin?

NOBBY: I'll flog the bloody thing.

WILLIAMS: Has diddums got a tender skin then?

NOBBY: Listen I'll bloody...

RADIO VOICE: Hello all Baker Baker Units. Here are today's numbers.

THISTLE: Numbers...

WILLIAMS: Ssh...

BIFFO: Where's my pencil?

WILLIAMS: Ssh...

RADIO VOICE: Eleven. One and one. Eleven.

ROWLEY: No.

BIFFO: Who's had my pencil?

WILLIAMS: Ssh...

RADIO VOICE: Twenty four. Two four. Twenty four.

WILLIAMS: Come on. Three weeks without a seven.

NOBBY: Think of his wife's appliances.

WILLIAMS: Bloody tender skin to you...

THISTLE: Ssh...

RADIO VOICE: One Seven. Seventeen.

WILLIAMS: Oh, no...

ROWLEY: Tremendous.

RADIO VOICE: Sixty three. Six and three. Sixty three.

THISTLE: Jesus wept.

NOBBY: Hey, did Biffo mention the Cherry B?

WILLIAMS: Look, I've warned you. Nobby...

NOBBY: It's the lad's future happiness.

WILLIAMS: If you...

THISTLE: Ssh...

RADIO VOICE: Fifty eight. Five and eight. Fifty eight.

WILLIAMS: Useless.

ROWLEY: Well, there's only one more Corporal.

RADIO VOICE: Thirteen. One three. Thirteen.

WILLIAMS: Thirteen?

RADIO VOICE: Thank you Baker Baker units. Today's numbers. Roger.

ROWLEY: Well that's our bad luck for today Thistle.

THISTLE: Aye.

ROWLEY: Might as well drive home for lunch.

THISTLE: Aye.

ROWLEY: Thank you Corporal.

NOBBY: Thank you sir. Nice to see you.

[*Exit ROWLEY and THISTLE.*]

WILLIAMS: I can still win you know.

NOBBY: Eh?

WILLIAMS: Turn it up again.

NOBBY: Why?

WILLIAMS: Because if anyone wins and phones in the RSM comes on air again.

NOBBY: You mean he says bingo on Brigade radio?

WILLIAMS: You know damn well that he says, reference today's numbers, affirmative response.

BIFFO: Affirmative response?

WILLIAMS: Yes.

BIFFO: Affirmative response.

NOBBY: Eh?

BIFFO: I've won.

WILLIAMS: You can't have.

BIFFO: I've got a full house.

WILLIAMS: Give it here.

NOBBY: Don't snatch.

WILLIAMS: Did you hear what he said?

NOBBY: Affirmative response.

WILLIAMS: I don't believe it.

NOBBY: Keep calm.

WILLIAMS: I am fucking calm.

   [*The phone rings. WILLIAMS snatches it.*]

   Ops. Room. If it's affirmative... What? Who are... [*To BIFFO.*] Rowley. Stop him at the OP...

   [*BIFFO cranks his phone link to the OP.*]

BIFFO: Sammy, Sammy...

WILLIAMS: Listen who are you and what...

BIFFO: Sammy. Stop Mr Rowley. Ask him back here...

NOBBY: It's not another fucking bomb is it?

WILLIAMS: [*writing.*] Ssh...

NOBBY: But what's happening?

WILLIAMS: Ssh...

BIFFO: You've got him? Great... Rowley's coming back.

WILLIAMS: Well...

   [*WILLIAMS puts his phone down.*]

   An hundred and seventy five quid.

BIFFO: Er... He's told Rowley.

WILLIAMS: Will there be a piss up for the lads?

BIFFO: Eh?

WILLIAMS: You heard.

NOBBY: He's not got the money yet.

WILLIAMS: What's in it for you? A Japanese motor cycle?

NOBBY: You're just hysterical because you haven't won.

WILLIAMS: If I am it's for that bastard Michael Donovan.

[*ROWLEY and THISTLE are in the doorway.*]

ROWLEY: Michael Donovan?

WILLIAMS: Yes sir.

ROWLEY: The real one?

WILLIAMS: Yes sir. Anonymous phone call. If you want Michael Donovan he's at Seventeen Rathcoole Gardens tonight.

ROWLEY: That's the Catholic Estate.

WILLIAMS: Yes sir.

THISTLE: It's very near the school actually sir.

NOBBY: Cheeky sods.

THISTLE: I've been on foot patrol in the early hours and smelled bacon and eggs from the bloody church.

ROWLEY: Shut up. Who was the caller?

WILLIAMS: A girl.

ROWLEY: Not a woman?

WILLIAMS: Well, eighteen or so...

NOBBY: It's always women that shop them isn't it?

THISTLE: Sometimes it's their mates in interrogation.

ROWLEY: Get me regimental Ops. Room.

BIFFO: Yes sir.

WILLIAMS: Reckon it's genuine this time?

ROWLEY: We must act as though it is.

NOBBY: Er... Biffo had full house sir.

ROWLEY: Biffo?

NOBBY: Yes sir.

THISTLE: An hundred and seventy five quid?

NOBBY: Aye.

THISTLE: Fuck me...

BIFFO: Bertie Platoon sir, will you hang on please...
Ops. Room, sir. Mr Fanshawe.

ROWLEY: Thanks... Hello Fanny it's Mike. Anonymous
phone call about our number one pin up boy... Yes.
Yes. I'll come over...

[*ROWLEY hangs up.*]

Thanks. Keep it among you three.

WILLIAMS: Yes sir.

[*ROWLEY and THISTLE go.*]

Michael Donovan. Shot while resisting arrest.

NOBBY: Eh?

WILLIAMS: Day dreaming.

NOBBY: You day dreamed that bloody seven. Coming
for lunch?

WILLIAMS: Oh God having it with you again.

BIFFO: Will you bring mine up?

NOBBY: No gravy.

BIFFO: That's right. Brenda's not phoned has she?

WILLIAMS: Oh bloody hell...

[*WILLIAMS goes.*]

NOBBY: She couldn't get through.

BIFFO: Are you sure?

NOBBY: Look how the phone's been going.

BIFFO: Aye...

NOBBY: No gravy.

[*NOBBY goes. BIFFO is left at the RT sets.*]

SCENE EIGHT

CUL-DE-SAC.

A desolate little cul-de-sac of garages on a Catholic housing estate like Ballymurphy. It is the middle of the night but there is still all the din of a riot.

[*KURT and FRITZ, the reporter and cameraman of a German television team run on busily filming the retreat of WILLIAMS, BIFFO and NOBBY who has the small radio.*]

WILLIAMS: Turn down there lads and we rejoin the road...

NOBBY: We don't you know.

[*KURT falls shot.*]

WILLIAMS: It's a bloody cul-de-sac.

WILLIAMS: It can't be.

NOBBY: It bloody is.

WILLIAMS: Well, in that case...

FRITZ: Excuse.

WILLIAMS: Hello.

FRITZ: My comrade gefallen is.

WILLIAMS: He's what?

BIFFO: He's fucking shot.

FRITZ: Gefallen.

WILLIAMS: Oh, no.

[*They cluster round KURT. FRITZ films them.*]

He's bloody filming...

NOBBY: Unconscious.

WILLIAMS: Was he shot here?

FRITZ: We along the roadway running were.

WILLIAMS: Yes. But was he shot here or down there?

FRITZ: I was the camera working.

NOBBY: Use your field dressing...

WILLIAMS: He's not our responsibility you know.
You're on this at your own risk, you do realise that
don't you?

[*Sniper's bullet comes very near.*]

Down...

[*All down. FRITZ on his feet.*]

Down...

[*FRITZ gets down.*]

That one cracked that did.

NOBBY: We're bloody trapped.

WILLIAMS: Shut up.

NOBBY: Get us out.

WILLIAMS: I'm thinking.

NOBBY: Cul-de-sac. Sniper laughing his head off.

WILLIAMS: Did you see his gun flash?

BIFFO: That's a dirty joke isn't it?

[*Another burst desperately near.*]

WILLIAMS: Got it.

NOBBY: Where?

WILLIAMS: Don't fire back. Block of flats.

BIFFO: There's no cover here at all.

WILLIAMS: Radio...

NOBBY: Bertie Three to Bertie Two. Bertie Three to
    Bertie Two. Do you read me? Do you read me?

WILLIAMS: What country are you from?

FRITZ: Germany.

BIFFO: Eh?

NOBBY: We need fucking Rommel here...

WILLIAMS: Shut up. There's cover up against that wall.
    When I say three Biffo you and me grab the Kraut.
    One, Two... Three...

[*Rush up taking KURT with them. FRITZ follows.*]

Phew...

[*Another bullet. Wider.*]

See? He can't get his angle.

[*BIFFO is settling KURT. FRITZ comes to look.*]

BIFFO: Television?

KURT: *Ja.*

NOBBY: Will you take the money or open the flaming box?

KURT: Boxing?

WILLIAMS: Listen...

BIFFO: It's gone quiet.

WILLIAMS: They've pulled the civvies back haven't they? Leave it to the snipers.

NOBBY: Bertie Three to Bertie Two...

WILLIAMS: Did your Brenda phone by the way?

BIFFO: Yes.

NOBBY: Bertie Three to Bertie Two...

WILLIAMS: What's happening?

BIFFO: She'll come to England won't she?

WILLIAMS: D'you think you've known her long enough?

BIFFO: I want to marry her don't I?

WILLIAMS: If you get out of here you mean?

NOBBY: Corporal...

WILLIAMS: What?

NOBBY: It's gone on the blink.

WILLIAMS: Look out...

[*Something thrown. Explosion.*]

Nobody hurt? Fucking nail bombs.

NOBBY: It's gone on the blink.

WILLIAMS: What?

NOBBY: Radio.

WILLIAMS: You mean you can't get through?

NOBBY: No.

BIFFO: We could be killed here.

WILLIAMS: Shut up.

BIFFO: We'll have to run for it.

WILLIAMS: Don't be daft.

BIFFO: I'm not daft. It's you that got us in here.

WILLIAMS: No, it isn't.

BIFFO: It bloody is...

WILLIAMS: Listen. We came out of the house and...

BIFFO: You bloody stupid bloody...

WILLIAMS: Don't speak to me like that.

NOBBY: Lads.

WILLIAMS: Shut up.

NOBBY: Lads... He's staring at you.

WILLIAMS: Eh?

NOBBY: Von Hindenburg.

BIFFO: Oh fuck him...

[*Another bullet.*]

WILLIAMS: Get in...

BIFFO: Oh no...

NOBBY: What's up?

BIFFO: I've pissed myself.

NOBBY: You've not.

BIFFO: I have.

WILLIAMS: We're a right smart lot then aren't we?

NOBBY: What d'you think happened to Mr Foster?

WILLIAMS: How do I know?

BIFFO: They will look for us won't they?

WILLIAMS: Of course they'll look.

FRITZ: Is kaput?

NOBBY: Yes, it's on the blink.

FRITZ: My friend a doctor needs.

WILLIAMS: All right.

NOBBY: He's got a night-sight on this camera.

WILLIAMS: You're bloody cheerful aren't you? We'll
    have to get a medic for him.

NOBBY: You said he's not our responsibility.

WILLIAMS: On paper he's not, but in practice...

BIFFO: Ssh...

WILLIAMS: Eh?

BIFFO: Funny noise.

[*They listen. It is someone a hundred yards away tapping
and blowing into a loud hailer to see that it works. Then
FATHER BOGAN's voice.*]

BOGAN: [*On hailer.*] Hello. Hello. British soldiers. Hello.

NOBBY: Who is it?

WILLIAMS: Listen...

BOGAN: [*On hailer.*] This is a priest. This is Father Tom
Bogan. Can I come through under a white flag?

WILLIAMS: You bet... [*Shouting.*] Yes. Come on. Yes.

NOBBY: White flag? How d'you know he won't throw
grenades?

WILLIAMS: Don't be daft...

BOGAN: [*On hailer.*] I am coming through now.

WILLIAMS: Step out Biffo and cover him.

BIFFO: Step out?

WILLIAMS: Oh, I'll go myself.

[*WILLIAMS stands out in the open.*]

NOBBY: Is he coming?

WILLIAMS: Yes.

NOBBY: Alone?

WILLIAMS: Yes.

BOGAN: ... [*calling.*] ...Hello. British soldiers.

WILLIAMS: Over here.

[*BOGAN arrives. He is holding a white towel in the air.*]

BOGAN: Are you Corporal Williams?

WILLIAMS: How d'you know that?

BOGAN: I've just talked with your officer.

BIFFO: I'm Catholic, Father. God bless you.

BOGAN: Bless you son. The people in the flats saw a
man fall. They think it was a TV reporter...

WILLIAMS: It was.

FRITZ: *Werfel. Sudbayischerundfunk.*

BOGAN: Is your friend a Catholic?

FRITZ: Of course.

[*BOGAN looks down to KURT.*]

NOBBY: He's unconscious.

BOGAN: I've made a deal with your officer. The ambulances come up for this man and you all withdraw.

WILLIAMS: Withdraw? We dominate this area.

BOGAN: You creep in at the dead of night.

WILLIAMS: How d'you expect us to come: with music?

[*BOGAN waving his torch as a signal.*]

BOGAN: The rumours say you were after Michael Donovan.

WILLIAMS: D'you know him?

BOGAN: Which one?

NOBBY: Very good. Which one. I like that.

BOGAN: What were you told? That Michael Donovan's mother lived in such and such a house and that Michael was to visit her?

WILLIAMS: Something like that.

BOGAN: The house was empty.

WILLIAMS: Yes.

BOGAN: What then?

WILLIAMS: The riot started.

BOGAN: So you were ambushed.

WILLIAMS: Well and truly.

NOBBY: Petrol bombs.

WILLIAMS: You should have seen it.

NOBBY: We got separated.

BOGAN: Who phoned the television?

WILLIAMS: Eh?

BOGAN: Our friends here...

WILLIAMS: Er...

NOBBY: You mean the IRA phoned them?

BOGAN: All I know is that when I ask the TV to film a story about homelessness or the school outing they tell me it's not news. Then tonight I'm knocked out of my bed by Mr Cahill of the Aid Association and here they are.

BIFFO: Mr Rowley's very good with the TV.

BOGAN: Is that a fact son?

BIFFO: Yes.

BOGAN: Thank you kindly.

[*Enter CAPTAIN ROWLEY.*]

ROWLEY: Right, father, thank you very much... Get that gentleman out of here will you.

[*KURT is lifted away.*]

You made a pig's ear of it didn't you?

WILLIAMS: ... [*Before he can speak ROWLEY sails on.*] ...

ROWLEY: Evening Fritz.

FRITZ: Mr Rowley.

ROWLEY: Who phoned you?

FRITZ: *Nicht verstehen.*

ROWLEY: Didn't think you would. Sorry about Kurt...

FRITZ: We meet soon for a drink?

ROWLEY: Why not? The bar of the Europa?

FRITZ: Gin and ton ton.

ROWLEY: Tremendous.

FRITZ: I think you will for many years here be.

ROWLEY: Me?

FRITZ: Soldiers...

ROWLEY: We'll beat them by the spring, Fritz. We'll destroy terrorism by the spring.

[*FRITZ bows and goes.*]

WILLIAMS: In actual fact, by not returning fire and thus not giving gun flashes to aim at, I saved our lives. How about a fucking medal?

ROWLEY: You made us look buffoons. Piss off.

[*WILLIAMS goes.*]

My God. A cul-de-sac.

BOGAN: I think we saved lives in it.

ROWLEY: I was in the house that Michael Donovan blew up.

[*BOGAN holds out his cigarettes. ROWLEY takes one.*]

BOGAN: Your boys say you're hot stuff with the TV.

ROWLEY: TV? Oh. I'm just the battalion publicity officer.

BOGAN: What's the secret?

ROWLEY: Sex and violence...

BOGAN: Aye, but it's how to use that for a good cause. Can we have a wee talk about it?

ROWLEY: I'm going home next week.

BOGAN: Will you be back?

ROWLEY: In the spring.

BOGAN: Oh you'll like that.

ROWLEY: Will I?

BOGAN: Oh yes. Our spring's just beautiful. It's very green.

[*BOGAN motions ROWLEY to go first. They walk down to the vehicle.*]

THE END

CORUNNA!

A Play with Songs

CHARACTERS

NARRATOR

BLACKER-ME-BOY

DRUMMY

JOHNNY TRAP

O'RIORDAN

LOMAX

SERGEANT MALHAM

SIR JOHN MOORE

MRS HUDSON

A SPANIARD

GENERAL COLBERT

A WEAVER

A RECRUITING SERGEANT

LORD HENRY PAGET

LIEUTENANT CADELL

A MANCHESTER MAN

WEAVERS, CAVALRYMEN, MANCUNIANS,
SAILORS etc

*The action of the play takes place in Spain and England
during the Napoleonic period.*

Corunna! was first performed by the English Stage Company at the Theatre Upstairs at the Royal Court on May 18 1971, with the following cast:

NARRATOR, Ashley Hutchings

BLACKER-ME-BOY, Brian Glover

SIR JOHN MOORE, Mark McManus

DRUMMY, Peter Knight

JOHNNY TRAP, Martin Carthy

LOMAX, Jack Shepherd

SERGEANT MALHAM/GENERAL COLBERT, Dave Hill

O'RIORDAN, Maddy Prior

MRS HUDSON, Juliet Aykroyd

LORD HENRY PAGET, Tim Hart

Other parts played by members of the company

DIRECTOR, Bill Bryden

DESIGN, Di Seymour

COSTUMES, Deborah Morris

MUSIC, Steeleye Span

ACT ONE

[The audience enters the show to a recording session situation in which tracks are being laid for the following:-]

INTRODUCTORY BALLAD: *The Mountains of Spain*

In the sweet flowering spring of the year Eighteen-
    Eight
Napoleon the bold marched his men into Spain
He said 'This land is mine now and all it contains!'
Slush snow rock for your bed
God it's cold the officer's dead
Face your front. Steady. Fire
In the hot dust of summer of the year Eighteen-Eight
We were sent by King George to fight Boney in Spain
For freedom and justice and honour's fair name
Ice. River. Haversack
Broken wagons. Night attack
Stand up. Look like men. Fire
In the cold of December in the year Eighteen-Eight
Having failed to stop Boney we had to retreat
Oh spare us Lord Jesus from the mountains of Spain
Frozen corpse. Prostitute
Burning village. Brandy. Shoot
Rearguard steady and fire
Oh spare us Lord Jesus from the mountains of Spain

[Throughout the play we use the band's front-man as our NARRATOR. He talks to the audience as he would at any show.]

NARRATOR: Ladies and Gentlemen – Sir John Moore.

[A chord or two of The British Grenadiers. *SIR JOHN MOORE appears like a massive cloaked statue risen from*

the ground. An impression of swirling mists and elemental forces. SOLDIERS and SERGEANT come on with him.]

MOORE: To give such account of myself as comprehension deems necessary:

I, John Moore, was born in Glasgow November 1761 the fifth child (and the third to live) of a respected and industrious physician. For services to the family of the Dukes of Hamilton my father was chosen in 1772 to travel with Douglas the eighth Duke upon his grand Tour of Europe, and since his Grace was a boy of little more than my own age I accompanied them. Later I was granted through the Duke's kindness a Commission in the Army. What influence procured industry and aptitude have furthered. In the present wars between England and France I have served in Corsica, the West Indies, Ireland (where we put down rebellion), the Low Countries, Egypt, Sicily, Sweden and Portugal. I have devised new drills and tactics for the British Infantry. I am a Knight of the Right Honourable Order of the Bath and Commander-in-Chief of His Majesty's forces in Spain. Yet I often think that the great world is little bigger than a Glasgow schoolyard. Consider the French Revolution, a mistaken upheaval which gave power not to the people but an enslaving tyrant Napoleon Bonaparte. Bonaparte is a school bully and Europe is his yard.

BLACKER: Bonaparte? We'll give him Bonaparte. We'll tear him apart.

SERGEANT: Thirty thousand foot: five thousand horse: first-class commanders and the whole Spanish army as well...

BLACKER: If we need them...

LOMAX: We're the best British army there's ever been. We'll thrash Bonaparte.

MOORE: They talked of going into Spain as of going into Hyde Park. Nobody seemed aware of what an arduous task it was, our commissariat is inexperienced and a scoundrel of a contractor has deceived us.

LOMAX: Just let us fight, that's all. Just put us face to face with Frenchmen.

MOORE: Bonaparte has taken Madrid. The Spanish armies are broken. The Spanish people have neither the power nor inclination to make further effort for themselves.

LOMAX: Let's fight. That's all. What if we are outnumbered? What of it?

MOORE: I advanced from Salamanca to Sahagun...

MEN: ... [*Cheers.*] ...

MOORE: Where we repulsed the army of Marshal Soult.

MEN: ... [*Cheers.*] ...

MOORE: My purpose was to bring against us the whole disposable force of the French. I succeeded. Bonaparte himself advanced upon us from Madrid.

BLACKER: This is it. Now we'll show 'em.

MOORE: Retreat.

MEN: Retreat?

MOORE: When it is proper to fight a battle, I will do it.

LOMAX: Bloody sodding hell. We've had no chance. We could have beaten them. Bloody useless... Bloody Spain... Bloody... We are bloody men you know.

SERGEANT: Keep in line there. Keep moving.

BLACKER: Shut up. Useless bloody orders.

[*By now SERGEANT and SOLDIERS have gone.*]

MOORE: My advance won some respite for the Spanish. England will be aroused by our retreat to the transports at Corunna; across a country without fuel, and at the most difficult season of the year...

[*Exit MOORE. Music starts: "Cold Haily Windy Night".*]

NARRATOR: Scene One. December Thirty First, 1808. The eighth day of the British retreat. Men of the rearguard, the crack 95th, have climbed the Manzanal Pass to the village of Combarros.

[*SERGEANT enters.*]

SERGEANT: Well done lads. Fall out. Ten minutes rest but keep your eyes peeled. There's nothing down that road but stragglers and the French.

[*As the MEN rest, the SERGEANT goes and the remainder of the song is sung. In the verse intervals the NARRATOR speaks to the audience.*]

NARRATOR: The 95th Foot was the best regiment in the newly formed Rifle Brigade. Its officers and sergeants have been vetted by Sir John Moore himself. Its common soldiers jeered at other infantry clodhoppers.

Riflemen were trained in scouting, fieldcraft, and other special skills. They were poachers and marksmen and they used not the old Brown Bess musket, but the Baker rifle, which had an accurate carry of 300 yards...

But don't go in the houses, lads, they're full of Spanish stragglers with typhus...

[*The THREE SOLDIERS of the Green-jacketed 95th are BLACKER-ME-BOY, a roughneck, JOHNNY TRAP, a man from the Shires, and DRUMMY, a slack-witted boy.*]

BLACKER: No surprise. I can smell 'em. Did you hear about Mrs Mackenzie?

NARRATOR: Mackenzie?

BLACKER: The wife of the Colonel of the 5th?

TRAP: No.

BLACKER: Got down. Urinated. Couldn't move.

DRUMMY: Eh?

BLACKER: Frozen solid to the ground, son.

DRUMMY: ... [*Looking from BLACKER to TRAP. Are they having him on?*]

BLACKER: It took three Irishmen to shift her. If I was you Drummy I'd get the sergeant off my back and crank that wind machine.

[*DRUMMY cranks the machine. Vicious blast of wind.*]

Cuts through you, don't it? Fall asleep in this snow and you don't wake up again. We should be out of here. There should be none of this hanging about for stragglers. Give me your scarf.

DRUMMY: Eh?

BLACKER: I'm cold.

TRAP: Hey – Blacker. Coming up the road.

DRUMMY: Jingle jangle pretty maids come jingle jangle...

BLACKER: Pretty maid's bum. I see her...

TRAP: She's in a bad way.

BLACKER: Johnny, I'm having first go at her and that includes first conversation. I'm a man and I know how to put a belt to them...

DRUMMY: Belts belts buckles and belts.

BLACKER: Lower your breeches. Look at your welts.
Understood, you rotten thieving poacher?

TRAP: I know what you mean; but she'll want me.

DRUMMY: Belts belts buckles and...

BLACKER: Belts. How much d'you wager?

TRAP: Blacker-me-boy: When we get home I'll take you
poaching: and you can hold a rabbity in your dirty fist.

BLACKER: How much?

TRAP: A shilling.

BLACKER: Done.

TRAP: I have first words, mind.

BLACKER: I say she'll walk past you.

DRUMMY: She's here. Pretty maid's bum.

BLACKER: Stand there, Johnny Trap, and let's see how
you philander.

[*JOHNNY TRAP and BLACKER take up their positions.
O'RIORDAN enters. She is singing to herself, rather
mechanically, to take her mind off her troubles.*]

O'RIORDAN: When I was sixteen I followed a soldier.
My heart was as white as...

[*O'RIORDAN stops singing when she sees the men but
keeps walking. She passes JOHNNY TRAP without looking at him again. BLACKER and JOHNNY control a
laugh as they register this fact.*]

BLACKER: ... [*About to open his mouth to speak.*]

TRAP: Are you tired, rabbity?

O'RIORDAN: What did you call me?

BLACKER: Wait a minute. She passed you.

TRAP: Rabbity. Would you like a cloth to wrap your feet in?

O'RIORDAN: I would. Are you the 95th?

TRAP: Drummy. Ask Blacker for your scarf, will you, and cut it in two?

DRUMMY: Er – Blacker...

BLACKER: Son – she walked past you.

TRAP: We are. We're the 95th. Will you walk with me?

O'RIORDAN: Why not?

BLACKER: Because he's broken the terms of the wager, that's why not. When I was in Newgate Jail I cut the throat of a girl your size.

O'RIORDAN: Well now you can cut that scarf, can't you?

TRAP: This is Blacker-me-boy.

BLACKER: I think she's a slag, son. I don't think she deserves a proper man.

DRUMMY: I stole that scarf in Salamanca.

TRAP: I'm Johnny Trap.

BLACKER: You're a poacher.

TRAP: We've survived more infantry fights than you've had hot dinners.

O'RIORDAN: I could eat one now.

[*In the village a cockerel crows. They can scarcely credit their luck.*]

BLACKER: Bloody hell. There it is. Roast chicken. Have we time?

TRAP: Course we have.

BLACKER: Usual procedure?

TRAP: You watch this, girl...

BLACKER: Fan out...

[*They creep stealthily into their cockerel catching positions.*]

O'RIORDAN: What the hell are you..?

BLACKER: Ssh.

TRAP: ... [*Clucks like a hen.*]

COCKEREL: ... [*Answering out of sight call.*]

[*BLACKER gives the thumbs up sign.*]

DRUMMY: Dunghill, dunghill I'm on top of the dunghill.

BLACKER: You'll be in it if you don't shut up.

TRAP: I'll bloody eat you.

COCKEREL: ... [*Answer.*]

BLACKER: He's still there.

TRAP: Ssh.

BLACKER: D'you like the dark meat or the white?

COCKEREL: ... [*Out of sight cry.*]

O'RIORDAN: I know that cockerel.

BLACKER: Eh?

O'RIORDAN: Lomax.

BLACKER: You'll scare him.

[*A man creeps in, bayonet poised, making cockerel noises.
He is PRIVATE LOMAX, in the red coat of The 20th.*]

O'RIORDAN: Lomax.

LOMAX: Eh?

TRAP: It's a bloody man.

LOMAX: O'Riordan.

O'RIORDAN: I've found him.

[*O'RIORDAN embraces LOMAX. The others stare. Then...*]

BLACKER: Son. Are those the facings of The 20th Foot?

LOMAX: Yes. [*To O'RIORDAN.*] We had to move out. Where were you?

BLACKER: You see? Twentieth Foot. Stinking sloppy useless yellow turds...

LOMAX: No we're not.

BLACKER: I'm a liar, am I?

DRUMMY: Belts out. Buckles and belts.

LOMAX: I make better cockerel noises than you.

BLACKER: Come on then.

LOMAX: Right. Three squawks apiece. You first.

BLACKER: Right.

[*BLACKER crows. Not very good. Sniggers.*]

LOMAX: I don't think he's breathing properly.

[*LOMAX crows. Magnificent. BLACKER is furious.*]

BLACKER: ... [*Crows again.*]

LOMAX: See. His breathing's constipated. He's not in my class.

BLACKER: I'm going to constipate you son.

O'RIORDAN: Can't you see he's wounded?

TRAP: Let 'em fight.

O'RIORDAN: Lomax...

BLACKER: Bloody Twentieth...

LOMAX: Leave me alone.

[*BLACKER rushes and hoists LOMAX above his head.*]

DRUMMY: Buckles and belts. Buckles and belts...

[*SERGEANT MALHAM intervenes.*]

SERGEANT: Rifleman. What are you doing?

BLACKER: Nothing Sergeant. He's from The 20th.

SERGEANT: Don't you know we're here to fight the French?

LOMAX: Then why don't we? Why don't we stop running and fight?

[*SERGEANT swings and punches LOMAX in the body.*]

Oh... you've opened my wound.

SERGEANT: Any more mutiny and I'll open your grave.

BLACKER: If I might say, Sergeant, since he is in that position, and knowing how you hate The 20th, what about my boot...

SERGEANT: ...up his...

BLACKER: Shit-hole.

SERGEANT: Yes, I never have had much time for The 20th.

[*SERGEANT turns ostentatiously away.*]

They're as useless as this weather. Keep hold of that woman.

[*TRAP grabs her. BLACKER prepares a running jump at LOMAX.*]

LOMAX: All I will say is that I believe in God's abounding grace.

[*As BLACKER kicks, SERGEANT wheels and catches his foot.*]

SERGEANT: D'you want to kick the pair of us?

BLACKER: Eh?

SERGEANT: Abounding grace. This turd's my brother Methodist.

[*He throws down BLACKER's foot.*]

You Midianite clown. Fall in. [*To LOMAX.*] March with me brother. Is this your wife?

LOMAX: Er – army wife, yes.

SERGEANT: Army wife?

LOMAX: ... [*A plea for silence.*]

SERGEANT: Spiritual difficulties brother? Wrestling in your bivouac with the bloody angel?

LOMAX: Yes.

SERGEANT: I have texts here brother. For she is my beloved and I am her's.

LOMAX: Set me a seal upon thy heart for love is stronger than death.

SERGEANT: Jealousy is stronger than the grave. Gathered your myrrh with your spices, have you brother?

LOMAX: Many waters cannot quench love nor the floods drown it.

SERGEANT: Eaten your honeycomb with your honey? Drunk your wine with your milk?

LOMAX: Well, now you come to mention it, yes.

DRUMMY: Listen...

[*They listen. Distant trumpets.*]

SERGEANT: That's your French trumpets. So move...

NARRATOR: It's the *Sabre Song of the French Cavalry.*

[*All sing the song, spoons etc. going for horses' hooves, and all jog up and down like men on horses. The tune is* The Marseillaise.]

[*Sabre Song of the French Cavalry.*]

Allez allez and oh mon Dieu
Cut off their heads and sacre bleu
Sabre them down trample them down
Allez allez pour l'Empereur
Nous sommes nous sommes the Lords of life
Up on a horse who needs a wife
Sabre them down trample them down
Helas bon soir and boule de suif.

FRENCH GENERAL: [*Heroic speech with music still going and riders still prancing.*] *Curassiers. Je suis le General Colbert et je vous accompagne – moi, et l'honneur de la patrie...*

[*Song continues.*]

Sabre them down trample them down
Sabre them trample them cut them down...

NARRATOR: Scene Two. That night Lomax and O'Riordan fell out of the line of march.

O'RIORDAN: Lomax. Can you go on?

LOMAX: Of course I can. I must.

O'RIORDAN: If I'd not found you again I'd have dropped.

LOMAX: What about those riflemen? You went with them quick enough.

NARRATOR: O'Riordan's song in the snow flurries...

[*O'Riordan's Snow Flurry Song.*]

When I was sixteen I followed a soldier
My heart was as white as the may
I thought that I'd die if ever we parted
My heart was as white as the may
But when in the field my lover was wounded
My heart was a cloudless new day
He died in my arms – I bedded another
My heart was a cloudless new day.

LOMAX: Just what I mean – bedded another.

O'RIORDAN: Lomax, when the regiment moved out
the other night I waited for you: but you'd already
gone, hadn't you? Did you want to lose me?

LOMAX: If I survive this retreat it's by will-power from
God. I must do right by those in England that I've
wronged.

O'RIORDAN: If you don't want me why are you jealous?

LOMAX: Leave me alone.

O'RIORDAN: I can't. I love you.

I fancied them rough, I fancied them bolder
My heart was a rover at play
Then I met you and with sad joy discovered
That I'd just been a rover at play...

[*NB: This linking passage which follows was put in to
cover the band's tuning-up and the necessity for it would
depend upon instrumentation.*]

NARRATOR: While we're tuning up you might like to
know that each rifleman had to carry on the march his
knapsack and straps, two shirts, two pairs of stockings,
one pair of shoes, ditto soles and heels, three brushes,
box of blacking, razor, soap tins and strap, an extra
pair of trousers, and a mess-tin, centre-tin and lid,
haversack and canteen, greatcoat and blanket, a

powder-flask filled, a ball-bag containing thirty loose balls, a small wooden mallet used to hammer the balls into the muzzle of his rifle, belt and pouch, the latter containing fifty rounds of ammunition, sword belt and rifle. Each squad had also to carry four bill-hooks, that weighed six pounds each, so that every other day each man had to carry it, in addition of course to his Fender Telecaster Guitar and Amplifier...

[*This following passage he says in any event.*]

As the retreat went on the soldiers' disappointment turned into rank indiscipline. Each day saw more desertion, drunkenness, and theft.

[*Band here sing "Wassail Song".*]

Scene three: January First 1809. The ninth day of the retreat. The rearguard reach the valley of the River Vierzo and the town of Bembibre, centre of the Galician wine trade.

DRUMMY: Blacker, what's happened? Are all these people dead?

SERGEANT: Dead drunk, rifleman. The entire army went berserk and smashed the wine vats.

[*Ballad of Bembibre Market Place.*]

Is that blood on the snow?
No it's liquor
Is that honour on the snow?
No it's piss
Are those laurels in the snow?
No they're curses
Brave lads I must lead you out of this.

BLACKER: It gets on my wick to see these men drunk when we've done all the bloody fighting.

TRAP: It gets on mine but what about it?

BLACKER: I say, stuff the army for an hour or two; stuff the war; let's find some drink of our own.

SERGEANT: Our orders are to rouse these stragglers.

BLACKER: Sergeant Malham, it's a stupid way to live is being shouted at by another human creature.

SERGEANT: Blacker, you – what are you doing?

[*BLACKER knocks MALHAM out with his musket.*]

BLACKER: Bastard. Look at the snotty hairs in his nostril. Ugly bastard.

[*BLACKER hits the SERGEANT again. His musket butt is about to fall a third time but TRAP stops him.*]

TRAP: Blacker...

BLACKER: Eh?

TRAP: Isn't he dead?

BLACKER: Bright red tears. Blood from his ears. Let's put him in a ditch.

TRAP: Bright red... Hey. We can run away if we like.

[*All giggle.*]

BLACKER: Bright red... I feel wonderful. Let's find a drink.

NARRATOR: Scene four. Several years previously. A flashback in which we see why Lomax joined the army.

LOMAX: Thank you. I, William Lomax, handloom weaver, came to be in the army because on that particular Thursday afternoon in question as I bent down to console my wife for the fact that we'd no work and prices were very high and the children were hungry – as I kissed her on the cheek, as you must do, thinking: Lord Jesus Christ why couldn't you have set before me a woman with a less pointed chin – as I bent over her and she gave me one of those pitying smiles, you know them, the sort that women do give to creatures who may in their own way be lovable but can't help being simple – as she did this and I resisted once again the temptation to butt her in the face I thought I caught on her breath – only thought mind you - what might be called a remembrance of spring onions. Now at our house we had not eaten spring onions for a week but I knew that they were flourishing in Walter Parkinson's side garden and –

[*Song. Unaccompanied hymn.*]

[*The other WEAVERS start to sing an unaccompanied hymn. LOMAX has to join in. Between verses he speaks to his neighbour.*]

My wife and that bandy-legged Walter Parkinson –

[*But the WEAVERS ignore him and launch into the next verse. In the next gap, he speaks again.*]

It's my belief that he's fucked her.

[*The other WEAVERS are scandalised but they sing the last verse.*]

WEAVER: Brother Lomax: take a text to thy mouth and wash it clean.

LOMAX: What are we doing here? No money. Slump in trade. Why are we singing hymns?

WEAVER: O Lord: our brother knows not what he doth.

LOMAX: All right. You explain why her breath had a distinct –

WEAVER: We, brother Lomax, look to our gracious Lord to bring us once again to family happiness and a boom in trade.

LOMAX: I'm walking down the lane to Manchester, where I hope to find someone who understands that I'm in mental bloody agony...

[*LOMAX turns away from the WEAVERS to the audience.*]

And I did. I found a recruiting sergeant.

[*The scene has become Manchester market place and the RECRUITING SERGEANT rides in to music.*]

R. SERGEANT: Roll up, roll up, roll up. Hold this horse my pretty maid, and we'll see about the oats later. Now listen to me, Manchester...

[*Recruiting Song of the Twentieth Foot.*]

Who wants to be a hero. Who'll join the Twentieth Foot. Who'll kiss the girls, who wants the loot. Who'll take this shilling and go. Roll up, now, who's married and unhappy? Who's out of work, who's a jailbird on the run, who lost his cottage when the landlord took his field; in short who wants to live boldly but life won't let him?

LOMAX: Me...

R. SERGEANT: Unhappily married?

LOMAX: Yes.

R. SERGEANT: Out of work?

LOMAX: Yes.

R. SERGEANT: Blind drunk?

LOMAX: Yes.

R. SERGEANT: Will you take it? Will you take the King's Shilling?

CROWD: Take it. Take the shilling lad.

LOMAX: Hang on. Do I get paid?

R. SERGEANT: Twopence a day.

LOMAX: How much does the officer get?

R. SERGEANT: He's like me. His comes in guineas.

LOMAX: But does he share the same hardships?

R. SERGEANT: Course he does.

CROWD: And he's a gentleman.

R. SERGEANT: He might be a lord.

LOMAX: Give me a shilling.

R. SERGEANT: For disobedience such as theft or drunkenness you get a hundred lashes.

LOMAX: Give me the shilling.

CROWD: Give him the shilling.

R. SERGEANT: You're in the army, son...

CROWD: Hurray...

LOMAX: Walter Parkinson – I'm a real man.

CROWD: Hurray.

[*All go out singing.*]

[*Recruiting Song of the Twentieth Foot.*]

You're in the army now, son
You're in the Twentieth Foot
So kiss my arse, kiss my boot
You've given your soul away.

NARRATOR: Scene Five. Bembibre again. In the middle of the afternoon Blacker wandered very drunk into the house of a merchant...

[*BLACKER, DRUMMY and TRAP are there, laughing and whooping.*]

... and with furniture and a cabinet of children's musical instruments and the wall hangings they made a fire on the tiled floor...

BLACKER: [*Warming himself.*] Oh that's better. Oh my God, that's better.

DRUMMY: No.

TRAP: Eh?

DRUMMY: I can play a fiddle. Hey diddle diddle.

[*DRUMMY salvages the fiddle which TRAP was about to throw on the fire. He looks round for a bow. BLACKER throws him one. DRUMMY plays a flourish.*]

BLACKER: Fanbloodytastic. Milady will you waggle your bum with me?

TRAP: We're too drunk, Blacker.

BLACKER: Are you threatening me?

TRAP: The French are coming...

[*DRUMMY starts to play a minuet.*]

BLACKER: We've got time for a bloody dance.

TRAP: All you are is a big mouth.

[*They both start giggling. Then DRUMMY strikes a chord and they take up their mock stately positions for* The Bembibre Minuet.]

I'll piss on you my Lord
You piss on me
I'll bow to you my Lord
You bend your knee
Up your Viscount my Lord
Tra la la le
For what you are my Lord's
A man like me.

[*LOMAX and O'RIORDAN are in the flickering shadows of the room.*]

LOMAX: That's not you is it Blacker?

BLACKER: Friend or foe?

LOMAX: Are you drunk?

BLACKER: As arseholes.

LOMAX: It's Blacker. Can we share your fire?

BLACKER: It's the bloody Twentieth.

DRUMMY: I thought they were dead.

BLACKER: I think he should be and then I could take my belt to his slag.

[*BLACKER grabs at O'RIORDAN but she has a bayonet.*]

LOMAX: If you're hungry we can offer biscuits.

BLACKER: Don't you snigger at me, son...

[*BLACKER knocks the bayonet out of O'RIORDAN's hand. She screams.*]

O'RIORDAN: Lomax...

LOMAX: I must return to Manchester and my true wife.

BLACKER: Don't snigger.

TRAP: Oh drink this and let 'em have a dance.

BLACKER: Eh?

[*DRUMMY plays. TRAP and O'RIORDAN dance. But then...*]

O'RIORDAN: I can't. My legs hurt. I need you, Lomax.

BLACKER: Let the 95th show you.

To men like us my Lord
The best is free
We have our place my Lord
A gallows tree.

LOMAX: If you need me why dance with them?

BLACKER: A gallows tree my Lord.
  A...

[*Fiddle stops.*]

BLACKER: What's the matter?

[*MRS HUDSON and SPANISH MAN are watching them.
They have come from within the house. MRS HUDSON
is very young and has an officer's pistol in her hand.*]

Drummy do you see before you in the fumes of the
wine vats an actual palpitationing Spanish Señorita?

LOMAX: I see death straggling along in the column. I
  must not fornicate again with O'Riordan.

MRS HUDSON: Palpitating.

BLACKER: Eh?

MRS HUDSON: Palpitating.

TRAP: Blacker...

MRS HUDSON: The word for which you seek is
  palpitating.

TRAP: She's English.

MRS HUDSON: Indeed I am. I am so excited that I
  scarcely know what I am writing. The words tumble
  from my pen...

BLACKER: She's bloody rambling.

MRS HUDSON: You know that men's glances have
  always fastened upon me; well, now I am married, to
  a Captain Hudson, at Bath, where dear papa had
  taken me in the expectation, nay, I should say the
  modest hope...

TRAP: Drink this rabbity...

[*TRAP gives her a drink.*]

Shall I mind the big gun?

MRS HUDSON: What? More wine?

[*TRAP takes the pistol and throws it to BLACKER.*]

TRAP: Who are you?

SPANIARD: Señor Caballeros. I am the steward.

TRAP: Cover him.

BLACKER: Who else is in there?

SPANIARD: Else?

O'RIORDAN: Lomax. I don't like it.

BLACKER: I'll look myself.

[*BLACKER goes to look.*]

MRS HUDSON: ...In the modest hope that I might
    there meet and form an attachment with a gentleman
    of suitable... Miss Marchbanks. Henrietta, my dearest.
    You are very young, I think... I have attended two
    other balls before this, sir.

DRUMMY: Look at her clothes. Silken bows.

O'RIORDAN: She's an officer's wife isn't she?

DRUMMY: Then why doesn't she talk sense?

[*BLACKER reappears with an officer's scarlet coat.*]

BLACKER: Her husband's in there. Bled to death. She's
    been waited on so much she can't even tie a proper
    bandage.

MRS HUDSON: Bearer party. You may carry the
    captain down. You don't look like the bearer party.

BLACKER: Deserted have they? Said they'd come back
    and didn't? Saved their own skins.

SPANIARD: *Si. Vamos.* Run away.

BLACKER: Shut up.

MRS HUDSON: Henrietta: you have your papa's great
fortune from the plantations. I have only my name, my
coat of arms, my dear old home and my commission.
All are yours if you will take them... Oh papa, I'm so
happy. How tall he is.

[*DRUMMY replies on the fiddle. She claps her hands.*]

Papa. Oh papa. I have been chosen. How childish I
used to be. Is such happiness possible?

O'RIORDAN: Come to me, love. I know what's in their
minds.

DRUMMY: ... [*Fiddle.*]

O'RIORDAN: Help me Lomax.

[*BLACKER hits O'RIORDAN.*]

Oh...

BLACKER: Up her viscount my lord and why shouldn't
I before I die out here? I've never had anything
beautiful. All we get is slummocks.

O'RIORDAN: Lomax.

LOMAX: If you want to live we must rest by this fire.

MRS HUDSON: I have negotiated the settlement, my
dearest, I account your love the greater... My head's
spinning.

DRUMMY: ... [*Fiddle.*]

MRS HUDSON: I have money. I can commend you to
your officers.

BLACKER: You can give me a kiss.

O'RIORDAN: Lomax...

LOMAX: I have a bad stomach wound missus but it won't deter me.

O'RIORDAN: Coward.

[*LOMAX grabs O'RIORDAN.*]

LOMAX: Sorry, love, but it's to keep us alive.

O'RIORDAN: Oh...

BLACKER: Why don't you throw another gilt chair on the fire, Johnny? And you come here.

MRS HUDSON: No. I have money. How dare you.

[*BLACKER tries to kiss MRS HUDSON. She bites him.*]

BLACKER: You bitch, you...

MRS HUDSON: Papa. Papa.

BLACKER: Get hold of her.

O'RIORDAN: Lomax.

MRS HUDSON: This grief: this dark overwhelming grief.

BLACKER: You're an officer's poke darling and we want our revenge.

TRAP: Blacker, what are you doing?

BLACKER: Eh?

TRAP: Have I not lain in the long grass and watched the ways of all creatures?

BLACKER: Are you going to hold her or not?

TRAP: Play...

[*DRUMMY starts the minuet again very quietly.*]

Why, there's the music for the ball already. Won't you come? Won't you show the town your pretty dress?

MRS HUDSON: But should I, so soon after...?

[*But TRAP has his arm out for hers.*]

Oh Lord. So many uniforms. So many brave gentlemen. Papa, I'm dancing, Papa.

A gallows tree my Lord
A rope of gold
Will you love me my Lord
When I am old
When I am old my Lord
And you are dead
I'll laugh at you my Lord
From my warm bed.

[*Laughter. BLACKER kisses MRS HUDSON.*]

MRS HUDSON: Gentlemen. Have you no shame, gentlemen?

BLACKER: None whatsoever.

[*As she laughs and drinks with them they dance her into the deep shadows of the room.*]

LOMAX: See that? Did you see it? That Johnny Trap poached her as easy as he poached you.

[*O'RIORDAN slaps his face.*]

Don't do that. I'm not your husband.

O'RIORDAN: You're not a man.

LOMAX: If you don't want me leave this fireside.

O'RIORDAN: I could say the same.

LOMAX: Oh... shut up and rest.

[*They rest. The SPANIARD creeps forward.*]

SPANIARD: Will they guess my secret? I am not the steward. I am the owner. This is my house: my furniture in ashes: my wine vats emptied: a dead officer on the floor of my late wife's parlour: excrement on the staircase, my neighbours robbed and beaten and now this... horror of war. Every law of nature and society upset by the rape of a virtuous and educated gentlewoman. Her noises excite me. Santa Maria. What depths of blackness in the human soul. I must think about something else. I can't. Yes I can. The vines. The vines are undamaged. Under the snow the vines are safe and yet every vat in the town has been smashed. Wine will be in very short supply. The next vintage will make us merchants astronomically rich...

[*Both we and the SPANIARD hear* The Sabre Song of the French Cavalry. *It forms an insistent background to the next scene which should be very noisy, rapid and confused. LOMAX and O'RIORDAN wake up.*]

LOMAX: French horsemen. They're in the street.

O'RIORDAN: What must we do?

[*The others are brought by this alarum from the shadows.*]

DRUMMY: I'm frightened.

BLACKER: Don't cling. I'm not dying for you.

SPANIARD: Hide in the cellar.

TRAP: I bloody told you.

O'RIORDAN: Get off your knees, Lomax.

LOMAX: Lord God Almighty do not kill me. I have a purpose...

TRAP: I told you we were drunk.

BLACKER: You fucked her as well.

DRUMMY: Other door. Find some more.

LOMAX: I must return to my wife and to my own responsibilities...

O'RIORDAN: Lomax.

BLACKER: Here...

[*BLACKER grabs the SPANIARD.*]

This is what we think of your country.

[*BLACKER stabs the SPANIARD.*]

TRAP: Save our skins.

DRUMMY: Not that way.

LOMAX: Amen Lord. Amen.

BLACKER: And this is for having to die in it.

[*BLACKER stabs the SPANIARD again.*]

DRUMMY: Come on...

[*MRS HUDSON appears.*]

MRS HUDSON: Help me, please help me.

DRUMMY: She wants help Blacker.

BLACKER: Let her husband help her.

[*BLACKER throws the officer's coat over MRS HUDSON's shoulders.*]

TRAP: We must find a way out.

MRS HUDSON: Silence.

O'RIORDAN: She's changed.

MRS HUDSON: Fall in. Move.

BLACKER: ... [*Running away.*] ... Well come on if you're coming.

MRS HUDSON: Rifleman.

BLACKER: Eh?

MRS HUDSON: Fall in.

[*Hesitation. LOMAX, TRAP and DRUMMY fall in. BLACKER joins them.*]

Stand up. Face your front.

TRAP: Sir.

MRS HUDSON: Rifleman?

TRAP: Your pistol, sir.

[*TRAP gives MRS HUDSON the pistol.*]

MRS HUDSON: Thank you. We will leave the house through the outbuildings. Follow me.

[*They all right turn and stand still in order of column. DRUMMY and BLACKER are at the back.*]

We will cross this square at the double for the cover of that parapet. At my word of command. Now.

[*They double. French see them. Start to chase and fire.*]

BLACKER: They've spotted us.

[*Whine of ricochets. DRUMMY falls. BLACKER jumps over him. The others are gone.*]

You bloody clumsy – you're not hit are you?

DRUMMY: No it's my bootlace.

BLACKER: Then get up and... don't bother. It's too sodding late. They've captured us.

[*BLACKER and DRUMMY smile in a sickly way and hold their hands up.*]

COLBERT: *Un deux. Un deux trois.*

[*Reprise of* Sabre Song of French Cavalry.]

Nous sommes nous sommes the lords of life
Up on a horse who wants a wife
Sabre them down trample them down
Allez allez pour l'Empereur...

[*BLACKER and DRUMMY are surrounded and taken prisoner.*]

INTERVAL

ACT TWO

[*The second half of the show begins with the band number* The Female Drummer.]

NARRATOR: Thank you. Scene six. Still Bembibre. Drummy and Blacker are brought for interrogation to the French General Colbert who was himself shot dead in action the next day.

[*DRUMMY and BLACKER are marched in to the Marseillaise.*]

Nous sommes nous sommes the Lords of life
Up on a horse who needs a wife
Sabre them down trample them down
Helas bon soir and boule de suif.

[*Next verse hummed as COLBERT makes sexy Boyer-type mutterings into his hand mike.*]

Allez and oh mon Dieu
Allez pour l'Empereur
Allez allez oh, oh mon Dieu
Allez pour l'Empereur.

[*COLBERT now makes his speech of self justification to the audience. From time to time he cannot resist making verbal love to one or another of the ladies within reach.*]

COLBERT: Women of the world, *je vous adore.* Citizens, *c'est moi,* your General Colbert who speaks. In this *histoire* am I not your representative? Do my soldiers not fight to bring about the modern world in which you live? The right of each man and woman to see their dreams come true. The achievement of happiness through obedience to the laws of science and of history. Who proclaimed these truths? Our French Revolution. Look at that thigh. I am as irresistible in the boudoir as in war. I must live each instant to the full.

[*COLBERT comes down to the ladies in the audience.*]

My goddess. I lay at your feet the ardour of a warrior, the devotions of a poet, the impatience of hot blood at the breast works. Your beauty is unflawed. Come tonight to my...

NARRATOR: General Colbert. Will you please return to the play.

COLBERT: *Alors*. The stern trumpet of my Country's need.

[*With some kissing of hands and sweeping of plumes COLBERT returns to the stage.*]

Citizens. Before our French revolution common persons could not behave as the glorious spirits took them... Your throat, my darling, the sweet valley between your... In 1789 in the name of liberty, in the name of equality, education and opportunity, French-men rose against their King crying: Let the modern world be born... Your eyes, my temptress, are smouldering pools in which a man may drown as he burns... and all over Europe the old Kings said no. In Austria, in Naples, in Sicily, in England, in Germany, in Russia and in Spain – wherever the beautiful life of the few depended on the subjection of the many, the old Kings said: the modern world must not be born. But it was: in the French revolution: in France: and to safeguard France is our Emperor Napoleon.

DRUMMY: Napoleon boney fat macaroni.

COLBERT: We executed our King.

BLACKER: That's not natural for a start.

COLBERT: We gave power to the people.

BLACKER: All them that didn't agree you guillotined.

COLBERT: We were invaded by the old Kings. We tossed them back... Toss me, my darling, upon the tiger skins... Now we invade, to take the modern world everywhere. Only England with her trade routes and her colonies and drunken scum soldiers can resist us. Oh perfidious England. She fights France across the globe and never once admits that her industrial revolution is a more devastating agent of the modern world than our Napoleon. Alors. This is illogical. It is the woman who to punish her husband will not have the orgasm.

BLACKER: Napoleon took power for himself and fought wars.

DRUMMY: Bloody dictator.

BLACKER: Course he is.

COLBERT: *Pauvre* thief. Pauvre half-wit. Their version of my epic is a drunken rape. But you... Oh *cherie*, if I had the time you could after the battle moan into my ear the glories of the individual life in your world. May you who are perfect remember the amorous General Colbert who fought for you. *Vive la Gloire.* It was for you that I evolved my policy as regards prisoners of war. To explain which I have made this speech. *Merci.*

[*COLBERT turns back into the play.*]

This man – cut out his tongue.

DRUMMY: No.

COLBERT: This man – his arm.

BLACKER: You can't do that.

COLBERT: Turn them loose at night among the enemy rearguard. This is the war of psychology.

BLACKER: No. I tell you what. We'll suck men off. That's what we'll do. We'll suck men off.

[*SOLDIERS cut out DRUMMY's tongue.*]

No.

[*SOLDIERS cut off BLACKER's arm and hold it up.*]

COLBERT: Long live happiness. Long live the lessons of history.

NARRATOR: Flash forward. 1972. *The Song of the Advertising Copywriter.*

Oh my adman's head is aching and my stomach's uptight
I need a glass of fizzing salts to put my bowels right
I feel unshaved and smeary
I feel sad and weary
On the charts in the health shop I'm a stone overweight
New York Special Filter King
New York Special Filter King
Washes Whiter Taller Walking
High Speed Instamated Zing.

For a really lively swinging time the obvious choice is Spain's Costa de Sol where Torremolinos sizzles away in the sun like a Mediterranean King's Road, Chelsea.

Oh my shirts are very trendy they cost ten guineas each
But I'm always uneasy what I want's out of reach
Mortgage, children and a wife
I'm tired of city life
In my dreams I run away and find an unknown beach
New York Special Filter King
New York Special Filter King
Washes Whiter Taller Walking
High Speed Instamated Zing.

NARRATOR: This very large lively hotel has its own ultra modern discotheque the Shalako, which is less than a year old, and has the dance floor suspended over the bar. To emphasise the carnival mood, the seats are arranged so that the whole place looks like a carousel.

Air crash horror many dead, and here's a tissue to blow
Just how certain are you that your husband doesn't know
In my polaroid glasses
I despise the masses
Your conversation bores me sweetie why don't you go
New York Special Filter King
New York Special Filter King
Washes Whiter Taller Walking
High Speed Instamated Zing.

As well as the largest swimming pool on the Costa Dorada, the hotel has two tennis courts, crazy golf, table tennis, horse riding facilities, bicycles and its own bull ring where guests who see themselves as toreros can take part in a mock bull fight with a young bull.

I took a first at Oxford of this shit I am ashamed

But if the masses want it baby why should I be blamed.

[MRS HUDSON and her stragglers have by now all entered.]

New York Special Filter King
New York Special Filter King
Washes Whiter Taller Walking
High Speed Instamated...

MRS HUDSON: Silence.

[Music stops. Silence.]

Twentieth. Ninety-fifth. Don't think. Live by your drill. Fall in. Quick march.

NARRATOR: Scene seven. January 2nd 1809. On the dusk road from Bembibre to Villafranca del Vierzo...

[*All in line. BLACKER, DRUMMY, SERGEANT with head bandaged, TRAP, LOMAX, O'RIORDAN, MRS HUDSON all struggling along.*]

MRS HUDSON: Sergeant. Let's hear them sing.

SERGEANT: Yes, sir.

LOMAX: Oh, bloody no...

SERGEANT: I want to hear it: every man and prostitute in cheerful bleeding voice.

[*TRAP leads them in Arthur Macbride. It quickens their pace and lifts their heads a little. Then as they march.*]

SERGEANT: Hey. Haven't we served together before?

BLACKER: Never.

SERGEANT: Are you sure?

BLACKER: Well: there was Egypt...

SERGEANT: No. Funny, because I could have sworn we...

TRAP: What happened? Crack on the head?

SERGEANT: Woke up wounded...

BLACKER: I'd say the man who did that had two arms.

SERGEANT: Very likely. How did your mate?

TRAP: Taken prisoner. This lad lost his tongue.

DRUMMY: ... [*Noise.*]

BLACKER: What we're fighting is beasts in human form.

SERGEANT: I'm afraid it gets beyond me since I was hit on the head. Somehow I've lost all my aggravation. I saw St Luke yesterday.

TRAP: Who?

SERGEANT: St Luke.

BLACKER: Oh, yes!

SERGEANT: Yes. Medical wagon. He'd lost his boots.

[*MRS HUDSON holds up her hand. They halt. There is something at the roadside.*]

BLACKER: What is it?

DRUMMY: ... [*Noise.*]

MRS HUDSON: It's a mother and child isn't it?

[*MRS HUDSON motions O'RIORDAN to look.*]

O'RIORDAN: Dead, sir. Frozen.

LOMAX: Amen.

SERGEANT: I put it to St Luke. I said what's the purpose of all this? No reply. Looked straight through me. There was ice on his beard.

O'RIORDAN: The baby's still alive.

MRS HUDSON: Pick it up.

LOMAX: We've no milk.

MRS HUDSON: Reform. March.

[*As they struggle along again LOMAX starts a hymn but they don't get very far with it. They hear a familiar noise and stop to listen.*]

TRAP: Cavalry.

BLACKER: Advance patrol.

O'RIORDAN: Haven't we suffered enough?

MRS HUDSON: Form up. Women and wounded to the rear... Are you the marksman?

TRAP: Yes, sir.

SERGEANT: Do I gather from that hymn, soldier, that you're a brother Methodist?

LOMAX: Indeed I am brother.

SERGEANT: I think I have met all you men before...

LOMAX: That hymn sounded in my ears on the best day in my life – the day I was totally immersed in the River Goyt...

SERGEANT: Total immersion?

MRS HUDSON: Face your front.

SERGEANT: You mean baptism into Christ's church by total immersion?

LOMAX: Total.

SERGEANT: That's blasphemy.

MRS HUDSON: Watch for them. Here they come. I want you steady against this charge.

SERGEANT: I could lose my immortal soul by kneeling with a total immersionist...

LOMAX: Are we not all brothers in the volley?

MRS HUDSON: Take aim...

[*HORSEMEN louder and nearer.*]

O'RIORDAN: They're bonny. Oh God but they're bonny.

MRS HUDSON: Fire.

[*Volley crashes out. Screams of wounded horses.*]

Marksman. The officer.

[*TRAP fires.*]

TRAP: Got him. [*Cheers.*] Blacker, we've thrown them back.

MRS HUDSON: Reload.

BLACKER: I'm tired son. It's getting dark, isn't it?

SERGEANT: Brothers in the volley. Very true. I never thought to be moved by an immersionist.

MRS HUDSON: Face your front.

O'RIORDAN: Sir.

MRS HUDSON: Get back woman.

O'RIORDAN: The baby's very cold sir.

[*MRS HUDSON looks.*]

MRS HUDSON: It's dead.

LOMAX: The Lord giveth and the Lord taketh away.

SERGEANT: Blessed be the name of the Lord.

LOMAX: Amen.

DRUMMY: ... [*Noise. Pointing.*]

[*They look down the road.*]

SERGEANT: That wasn't the patrol It was the outriders of a column.

BLACKER: That's it then. Sodding death: I'm not sorry.

MRS HUDSON: Silence. Fall in. It will very soon be dark. One man must volunteer to fight a rearguard.

[*TRAP steps forward.*]

DRUMMY: ... [*Noise. He knows it means death.*]

SERGEANT: You can't make him, sir.

[*MRS HUDSON takes the baby from O'RIORDAN and gives it to TRAP.*]

MRS HUDSON: His conscience makes him. Right turn, quick march.

[*MRS HUDSON marches them off. TRAP is left with the baby.*]

TRAP: The ground's too hard to dig your grave little rifleman, so what we'll do is collect all these cavalry pistols, and I'll fire 'em off with one hand and hold you with the other.

[*TRAP settles down.*]

Don't be afraid when we come to the river. It's not like these mountain torrents. It's an English river so I know how to cross. It has water meadows a bit squelchy and slushy at the bank and on the far side there are willows. I like a pollarded willow... Hey, who was your father I wonder and what country? Don't fret yourself. When you're in the army (and you are, you're an army baby) when you're in the army you must learn to sleep anywhere.

[*JOHNNY TRAP's Lullaby.*]

Sleep, sleep, though the
Bugles complain
Sleep, sleep. Sleep
Steady in Spain
Sleep, little rifleman
Sleep through the volleys
Sleep, little rifleman, sleep Johnny Trap
For you won't see the green leaves of England again
Sleep steady, sleep steady
Sleep steady in Spain
For you won't see the green leaves of England again.
Here they come sonny. It's an English river. Hold me.

[*Music. And noise of French cavalry. Lights fade.*]

[*The figure of SIR JOHN MOORE appears again, watching his troops struggle along.*]

MOORE: I would not have believed, had I not witnessed it, that a British army could in so short a time have become so completely disorganised. Its conduct along the late march has been infamous beyond belief. I can say nothing in its favour except that where there was a prospect of fighting the enemy, the men were orderly and seemed pleased and determined to do their duty. I am, sirs, your obedient servant. January 13th 1809.

O'RIORDAN: Lomax. I'm falling.

LOMAX: Then you won't see me again.

O'RIORDAN: Lomax...

[*LOMAX keeps moving.*]

Lomax.

[*LOMAX stops and turns.*]

LOMAX: Get up.

O'RIORDAN: I can't.

[*Wind. LOMAX is forced to his knees.*]

LOMAX: I need you. I bloody well need you.

O'RIORDAN: You need your wife in Manchester.

LOMAX: Will you get up?

O'RIORDAN: Help me.

LOMAX: You must help yourself.

O'RIORDAN: Will you watch me die if I don't?

LOMAX: Oh. I've got strength, don't worry. I'm hard, me, I'm hard. I'm... All right, I will not go back to my wife.

O'RIORDAN: Do you swear it?

LOMAX: I swear; so will you get up?

[*O'RIORDAN gets up.*]

O'RIORDAN: Yes...

NARRATOR: Scene seven. Mrs Hudson rejoined her stragglers to the main body at Villafranca del Vierzo and reported to Lord Henry Paget, the heir to vast estates, and commander of the rearguard.

[*PAGET has a bandage round his eyes, and his EQUERRY is dressed in a blanket.*]

MRS HUDSON: Remnants of the Twentieth and Ninety-fifth, my lord.

PAGET: My dear lady, you must forgive this absurdity. I have an infection of the eyes. This is my equerry, Lieutenant Cadell.

MRS HUDSON: Sir.

CADELL: Will you be seated, Mrs Hudson?

MRS HUDSON: Thank you.

PAGET: I understand that you have incurred personal sorrow. I knew your husband well, and admired him: and as for the assault upon your person...

MRS HUDSON: I have made my report, my lord.

CADELL: May I take your coat Mrs Hudson?

MRS HUDSON: Coat?

[*CADELL takes off her uniform coat. When it is removed she starts to scream. They don't know what to do. The noise goes on. PAGET motions. CADELL slaps her. She stops screaming.*]

MRS HUDSON: Papa, I have been chosen, papa. I have been chosen.

PAGET: My poor, dear lady.

[*MRS HUDSON's sings her* Rocking Horse Song.]

Rocking horse, rock your head
I'll tell you a secret
This is what she said...
Buttercup pressed between
Pages of my diary
Secret, secret, ssh...
Nursery rainy day
I'll tell you a secret
Clouds will roll away...

PAGET: I will give you a cavalry escort Mrs Hudson,
and whatever else is possible.

MRS HUDSON: To ride prettily among tall men and
plumes.

PAGET: Was that why you came to Spain?

MRS HUDSON: Yes.

NARRATOR: Scene eight. The execution by firing
squad of Blacker-me-boy, for the rape of Mrs Hudson,
in cold rain at Villafranca del Vierzo.

SERGEANT: By the left, quick march. Squad halt.
Prepare to fire. Aim.

BLACKER: All you in England are shithouse bastards.

SERGEANT: Fire.

[*Volley. BLACKER is dead.*]

MRS HUDSON: There is no satisfaction in his death. I
am left with nausea and disgust. I am persuaded
sometimes that the lower parts of my body have
grown scurf like leathern scales and that the flesh
around my orifices is not tender but a crust and that

what trickles there is puss. For days we have ridden to
Corunna in worsening conditions and yet I welcome
the cold. I wish to apply it to the furnace of my body.

[*SIR JOHN MOORE sees MRS HUDSON.*]

MOORE: You return on the packet, Madam, may I give
you God speed...

[*The shanty* A Hundred Years Ago *gets MRS HUDSON
aboard.*]

MRS HUDSON: It was aboard the packet that I discovered from the monthly miracle of nature that I was
not with child of any sort of fatherhood: which news
with the salt spray initiated the revival of my spirits...
Weightier intelligence was not long to follow us, that
before the embarkation of his army Sir John Moore
gave battle at Corunna. In the moment of victory he
was knocked from his horse by a round shot. His left
breast and shoulder were quite shattered and the gold
thread of his lapel driven deep into the wound. At
evening he died.

[The Burial of Sir John Moore *by Charles Wolfe, is now
delivered by a member of the burial party.*]

Not a drum was heard, not a funeral note
as his corpse to the rampart we hurried;
Not a soldier discharged his farewell shot
O'er the grave where our hero we buried.
We buried him darkly at dead of night,
the sods with our bayonets turning,
By the struggling moonbeam's misty light,
and the lantern dimly burning.
No useless coffin enclosed his breast,
Not in sheet or in shroud we wound him;
But he lay like a warrior taking his rest,
with his martial cloak around him.
Few and short were the prayers we said,

and we spoke not a word of sorrow;
But we steadfastly gazed on the face that was dead,
and we bitterly thought of the morrow.
We thought, as we hollowed his narrow bed,
and smoothed down his lonely pillow,
how the foe and the stranger would tread o'er his head,
and we far away on the billow.
But half of our heavy task was done,
when the clock struck the hour for retiring;
And we heard the distant and random gun
that the foe was sullenly firing.
Slowly and sadly we laid him down,
from the field of his fame fresh and gory;
We carved not a line, and we raised not a stone,
but we left him alone with his glory.

[*From a great distance we hear the fiddle of a jig approaching.
It brings on DRUMMY, LOMAX AND O'RIORDAN.*]

NARRATOR: Scene ten. Years later. After another
British army had been sent to Spain and under the
Duke of Wellington had brought down Napoleon: the
soldiers come home...

[*Playing and dancing.*]

LOMAX: Wounded victims of the war, gentlemen.
Dance along with the victims, madam... [*Looks at the
coin.*] Bitch...

[*They stop the music.*]

O'RIORDAN: Lomax. Where is this?

LOMAX: I'm not sure.

O'RIORDAN: What d'you mean?

LOMAX: Leave me alone.

O'RIORDAN: What was it you used to tell me about the
place where you lived with your wife? There was a

lane with hawthorns, and at the bottom of the lane, Manchester...

LOMAX: Yes.

O'RIORDAN: Just as Manchester's at the bottom of this hill we've walked up.

LOMAX: Well...

DRUMMY: ... [*Fiddle.*]

LOMAX: I know. The hawthorns have gone. Factories... Smoke. I can see for myself.

O'RIORDAN: You promised me that if we ever had to pass through Manchester we'd go nowhere near the place where you used to...

DRUMMY: ... [*Fiddle.*]

LOMAX: Shut up: the pair of you. I've noticed the people myself. I can see there's something wrong with them.

O'RIORDAN: Have you broken your promise or not?

LOMAX: Yes. I mean no. I mean... It's changed... I mean, I'm human, woman. I've got more curiosity than sense.

O'RIORDAN: I've got your three children.

LOMAX: I only want one look from a distance.

DRUMMY: ... [*Fiddle.*]

LOMAX: What d'you mean? How distant?

O'RIORDAN: Don't shout at him.

LOMAX: I'm not shouting. I'm... All right. I'm a fool. I wanted to see my past life. See how clever I'd been at escaping: see whether I really had been clever.

O'RIORDAN: You fool.

LOMAX: All we are is street beggars.

DRUMMY: ... [*Fiddle.*]

LOMAX: Yes we are. But what I find here is this smoke and factories and... Wait a minute. This is where my uncle lives.

[*A MAN appears.*]

LOMAX: Er – excuse me.

MAN: There's no work here.

O'RIORDAN: We were with the Duke of Wellington.

LOMAX: We brought Boney down, sir.

MAN: Well, there's no work here, so clear off.

LOMAX: This is my uncle's house.

MAN: No it's not. It's my warehouse.

LOMAX: Warehouse?

DRUMMY: ... [*Fiddle.*]

O'RIORDAN: Ssh... I know the man's a bastard.

LOMAX: Does Mrs Lomax live three doors along?

MAN: Three doors along has been pulled down.

LOMAX: My God they have.

MAN: Clear off. I don't like the look of you.

LOMAX: Sometimes we'd have to wait to go into battle, sir, we'd lie on our backs in the long grass; funny little insects you notice, don't you, and you notice things about yourself. It's very warm. Your sweat starts as one single blob in your armpit, and then swish, sir, you see earth spatter; you see cannon balls bounce along – oh, they do actually bounce, sir, it's very comical. I've seen them tear men to pieces. I've had my best pal's intestines all over my uniform, I've done things that you wouldn't credit, and after a day of that long grass, I've been screaming inside I can tell you. I've heard hundreds of men screaming with their mouths shut. If there'd been no battle to fight we'd have burst.

MAN: If a man can't work, he's immoral and useless and he doesn't deserve to be supported by the rates.

LOMAX: There is no handloom work. It's these machines.

MAN: Move, or must I fetch the constable?

LOMAX: Sir. Dear brother in Christ. I can hear your scream. Why can't you hear mine?

MAN: I'm not obliged to listen to blasphemy.

[*MAN goes.*]

LOMAX: But we fought for you, sir. The officers told us that we were fighting for the liberties of old England. Not that I personally ever had many. It was the start of this machinery that put me out of work, then one thing and another happened and – when you've no work you shrink. Your private parts shrivel. You're not a man. Hard to believe if you've not known it, but – then I took the King's shilling and I was a man again of a sort, but when I look at these people leaving the factories, when I see the people here who have got work – are they men? Is this old England's liberty? Discharged from the army with no dole. Naked women in the coal mines. Little girls in the cotton machinery.

[*To the audience.*]

Look at you. Look at you factory people. You're screaming inside.

[*Back to O'RIORDAN.*]

What was it like before, O'Riordan? What was the
other England like? I can't bloody remember.

[*Again to the audience.*]

It was all green wasn't it, the England that we fought
for?

[*O'RIORDAN answers him with the song* The Lark in
the Morning. *During the song the NARRATOR speaks
to the audience.*]

NARRATOR: When the Napoleonic wars ended in 1815,
there was a boom followed by a much longer slump.
There was great hardship in the new industrial areas
and great radical agitation. At Peterloo in 1819 cavalry
sabred down the crowd... Then trade boomed and
grievances were forgotten until the next slump and
people began to make their own private peace with
the modern world.

[*When the song ends the lights fade.*]

[*Then the lights come up again and the band plays a jig to
which the actors take their bows and dance off.*]

THE END